Edinburgh Bilingual Library (9)

Cenodoxia = vain-glory (Gal. 5:26; Phil. 2:3)

EDINBURGH BILINGUAL LIBRARY (9)

see pp. 18, 9ff 24

Cenodoxus

(a moral play on stubborn pride vs. religious vows.

(1602) (augsburg) Good introd. – relates to

JACOB BIDERMANN

Renaissance theatre (Faustus, Everyman, Hamlet, etc.) + to stoicism vs. Xtianity

EDITED AND TRANSLATED BY

D. G. DYER

Fellow of Exeter College, Oxford

JOINT-TRANSLATOR
CECILY LONGRIGG
Lecturer in English,
St. Hilda's and St. Anne's Colleges, Oxford

UNIVERSITY OF TEXAS PRESS, AUSTIN

International Standard Book Number 0-292-71028-3
Library of Congress Catalog Card Number 74-15527
Printed in Great Britain by
    W & J Mackay Limited, Chatham, Kent

Edinburgh Bilingual Library

FOREWORD

An imperfect knowledge of a language need be no bar to reading a work written in it if there is a good translation to help. This Library may aid those who have a wide-ranging and adventurous interest in literature to jump the hurdles of language and thus do something to help break down the barriers of specialization. That it may be helpful for courses in Comparative Literature is our hope, but not our main aim. We wish to appeal to a wider audience: first to the cultivated, serious reader of literature who is not content to remain within the English language, secondly to university students and teachers of English and of Modern Languages by inviting them to throw from outside some new light on, perhaps even discover different values in, their particular fields of specialization.

The languages represented will be French (with Provençal), German, Italian, Portuguese, Spanish (with Catalan), and Medieval and Renaissance Latin. The translations will not be 'cribs' but good literature worth publishing in its own right. Verse will generally be translated into verse, except where the unfamiliarity of the language for most readers (Provençal, Catalan, Old French, Old High German) may make a more literal prose rendering advisable. In the majority of cases the Introductions will present up-to-date assessments of each author or work, or original interpretations on a scholarly level. Works already accessible in translation will be included only when we think we can offer a new translation of special excellence or when we wish to relate it to another volume in the series.

As this Bilingual Library grows it will attempt to map, in a necessarily limited and modest way, small areas of Western Literature through the comparison of actual texts. This it will hope to do by building up groups of volumes to illustrate literary traditions, themes and styles. Thus no. 3, *Troubadour Lyric Poetry*, will be followed by volumes of Petrarch, Ausias March and others, which together will chart the range and significance of Courtly Love. From time to time volumes will be paired to show literary developments across countries and periods, although simultaneous publication will not always be possible. *Die Nachtwachen des Bonaventura* (no. 6) and Valle-Inclán's *Luces de Bohemia* will show how pessimism and despair in German Romanticism could foreshadow the twentieth-century literature of the Grotesque. Bidermann's *Cenodoxus* when read with Tirso de Molina's *El condenado por desconfiado* will show how Jesuit school drama gave rise not only to the martyr plays of seventeenth-century Europe, but to a whole dramatic genre in Spain—the *comedia de santos*.

A. A. Parker, GENERAL EDITOR

Acknowledgment
We would like to express our grateful thanks to M.D. Reeve, Fellow in Classics at Exeter College, Oxford, for the unflagging help he has given us with this translation.
D.G.D. and C.L.

Contents

Cenodoxus
Jacob Bidermann

INTRODUCTION

Cenodoxus, sive Doctor Parisiensis was first performed on 3 July 1602 in the small hall of the Jesuit college at Augsburg. The performance lasted for four hours, and the play was so well received that it had to be repeated on the following day. It was produced again in Munich in 1609 in a performance that was one of the most noteworthy recorded in the history of the Jesuit college there. Munich was a stronghold of the Jesuits. When Bidermann went there the college, founded in 1559, boasted close on a thousand pupils, the sons of wealthy and influential persons, and the college records are full of visits from illustrious princes and nobles. It was the custom in Jesuit colleges to produce a play on the occasion of the annual prizegiving. Whilst at Munich Bidermann was entrusted with the task of producing these plays, and in this he achieved such success that for a time he completely dominated the Jesuit stage there, which had risen above the level of a local college theatre and become the court stage of Munich. A distinguished audience, graced with the presence of leading nobles, attended the theatre, and it was clearly in the interests of the Jesuits that their plays should have a maximum impact on so influential an audience. This the 1609 performance of *Cenodoxus* clearly had. The hall was packed with an audience which included important nobles of the Bavarian court and the foremost citizens of Munich. At first the audience rocked with laughter at the opening comic scenes; but as the play progressed the mood changed to one of shock and horror as the spectators realised the enormity of the sins portrayed and became aware of the power of hell; and by the end of the play the members of the audience, trembling at the sight of a soul eternally damned, were reflecting in stunned silence on the punishment their own sins merited. The impact of the play was immediate. Fourteen members of the audience went into retreat to perform the Spiritual Exercises of St Ignatius, just as in the play Bruno retreated into the wilderness to found his monastery and lead a life of spiritual contemplation; and the actor who played the part of Cenodoxus shortly afterwards entered the Society of Jesus and after a life of piety and holiness died in the odour of sanctity. Such was the effect of *Cenodoxus*. In a few hours the play had accomplished what a hundred sermons could hardly have done.[1]

Cenodoxus, in common with other Jesuit plays, was written in Latin. It may at first sight seem strange to modern readers that the play was written in Latin, a dead language, and that it could have such an effect on the audience. It is important to realise that when the play was written Latin was by no means a dead language, but that it had survived the fall of the Roman Empire and had been in constant use as a means of communication, both oral and written, from then until Bidermann's time. Throughout the Middle Ages Latin was the language used by the Church, by scholars and educated people, and was the vehicle for a vast amount of literature, much of which survives and is read today. Mediaeval Latin acquired in the course of time a character that was very different from the Latin of classical writers, whether it was the Latin of a St Thomas Aquinas, classically based, but enriched by the terminology of dogmatic theology and sharpened into the subtle and refined vehicle of scholastic argument or then the Latin of wandering students, court officials, chroniclers and monastic scribes, a racy vivid 'dog' Latin that, while hardly satisfying the strict canons of classical Latinity, was the esperanto of people throughout the civilised world.

With the rediscovery of classical antiquity heralded by the Renaissance and the spread of humanistic studies throughout Europe a great impetus was given to the cultivation of a Latinity that could vie with that of the Ancients. Writers and poets were at pains to develop a pure Latin style and modelled themselves on classical Latin authors whom they sought to emulate and even surpass. The advent of the Renaissance and the renewed interest in classical authors led to the re-discovery of classical poetic forms and helped stimulate interest in the burgeoning genres of modern drama and the modern novel. When educated men of the day turned their hands to writing poetry, plays, satires and prose works it was natural that they should write in Latin, the standard means of international communication and a ready-made and polished linguistic medium capable of a wider and more sophisticated range of expression than the vernacular languages at that time, many of which were still undergoing the metamorphosis from mediaeval to modern forms. Gradually a considerable body of neo-Latin literature built up during the sixteenth and seventeenth centuries, much of it work of considerable distinction. The works of Erasmus, for example, were widely read throughout Europe and these included, apart from his biblical and exegetical studies, the famous *In Praise of Folly* (*Moriae Encomium*, 1509, with the punning allusion in the title to his friend Sir Thomas More), the immensely popular *Colloquies* (1519) and the moving testimony to the ideal Christian soldier in the *Enchiridion militis christiani* (1502). Innumerable poets wrote elegant Latin verses exploiting a wide range of classical metres, one of the most distinguished being the German poet Conrad Celtis (1459–1508), known as the 'German archhumanist' and the first poet-laureate ('poeta laureatus') of Germany. A best-seller in its day was the neo-Latin satire *The Letters of Obscure Men* (*Epistolae obscurorum virorum*, 1515–17), a pungent and highly readable defence of the German humanist Johannes Reuchlin against those who challenged his enlightened humanism. One of the most famous works in the field of the novel was the *Argenis* (1621) of John Barclay (1582–1621), a satirical tale of adventure and romance owing something to Petronius and a work frequently attacked by earnest moralists because of its supposed immorality. In the field of drama too there was a great deal of activity on the part of neo-Latin writers. Plays in Latin on secular and biblical subjects were written by writers as far afield as Scotland, Scandinavia, Spain and Hungary, and these plays, based as they were on the comedies of Terence and Plautus and, later, the tragedies of Seneca, contributed greatly to the development of European drama. With their classical five-act form and with the concentration and conciseness resulting from the fact that they were performed before a restricted audience on an indoor stage they represented a radical break with the mediaeval mystery and morality plays and the open-air spectacles that had until then constituted much of the vernacular drama. Latin school-dramas, written by scholars, teachers, priests and clerics for public edification and entertainment and performed by pupils who spoke Latin as a matter of course, in colleges and schools, on stages erected in courtyards and halls became increasingly popular during the course of the sixteenth century. At Strassbourg, for example, a particularly noted centre for such plays, the lavish and sophisticated productions of Latin plays in the Hof-Theater were watched by up to two thousand spectators at a time. Most of the plays were of no particular literary merit, written for a special occasion and soon forgotten. But some stand out above the rest and can still be read with enjoyment and admiration today, notably *Acolastus* (1528), a play dealing with the theme of the Prodigal Son by Guilhelmus Gnapheus (1493–1568), *Hecastus* (1538), an Everyman-type play by Georgius Macropedius (1485/6–1558), and *Euripus* (1548) by the Franciscan Levin Brecht. Thus it was that in all fields neo-Latin literature flourished. Far from being a disadvantage the fact that it was written in Latin worked to its advantage, for it meant that it could be read throughout Europe by the many people for whom Latin was not a dead but a living language.

From the end of the fifteenth century plays were written in Latin, and neo-Latin drama flourished. From the middle of the sixteenth century onwards Latin drama was dominated for a century and a half by the drama of the Jesuits.

The Society of Jesus was founded by St Ignatius and officially sanctioned by Pope Paul III in the papal bull of 27 September 1540. Its object was the propagation and strengthening of the Catholic faith, and one of the main means employed to this end was educational activity at all levels. Colleges were founded throughout Europe and in countries overseas where the sons of Catholics, and not only Catholics, were educated. By 1587 there were 148 Jesuit colleges in Europe. By 1626 there were over 100 colleges and academies in German-speaking lands alone, and by 1725 this number had risen to 208. Some of these colleges, where Latin was regularly spoken, attracted a large number of pupils. The college at Cologne had nearly 800 pupils in 1558, that at Münster had almost 1400 in 1617, and in 1631 the college at Munich boasted 1464 pupils. The Jesuits, who were excellent and highly progressive educators, soon realised that the theatre was eminently suited to religious propaganda, as can be seen from the fact that the 1609 Munich performance of *Cenodoxus* was reported to have accomplished in a few hours what it would have taken a hundred sermons to do. It became the custom to perform plays in Latin on suitable occasions, and by the end of the sixteenth century plays were regularly performed in the colleges to mark the annual prize-giving, to honour the visit of a high dignitary, to commemorate the festival of a patron saint and to celebrate the founding of a new college or the consecration of a new building. The Jesuit theatre quickly established itself and played a leading role in the development of European drama. It is hardly an exaggeration to say that virtually all leading seventeenth-century dramatists outside England were influenced directly or indirectly by the productions of plays on the Jesuit stage. A Jesuit father, usually the Professor of Rhetoric, would be appointed 'choragus' and given the task of producing the play, which he would normally write himself. The play would be written in Latin, but summaries in the vernacular ('periochae') would be distributed to enable the audience to follow what was happening. The plays drew on a wide range of subject matter. Some were written to show the bad effects of unchristian behaviour; some dealt with significant events in the history of the Church; some portrayed the lives of Christian saints and martyrs; some dealt with the Four Last Things (death, judgement, hell and heaven) and showed the wiles of Satan and his hosts; and some engaged in polemic and expounded the dogmas of the Catholic Church. Not infrequently the plays combined two or more of these themes. Written on the model of classical five-act dramas, the plays were constructed in such a way that the action culminated in a climactic closing scene that made the greatest possible impact on the audience. These plays fulfilled an important function in propagating Catholic doctrine and countering the effects of the Reformation; but they also served to give the Jesuit pupils practice in spoken Latin and generally train them in declamation and deportment, thus fitting them for the public careers for which they were destined. The productions were extremely popular and were visited by all sections of the population, and in writing his play the choragus took care that it was geared to appeal to all classes. Productions were lavishly staged, particularly at Munich, the spoken word being embellished with music and dancing, and as the seventeenth century progressed the introduction of ballet and operatic elements meant that something approaching a 'Gesamtkunstwerk' was achieved. Every means was employed to gain maximum impact; and this impact the 1609 Munich performance of *Cenodoxus* clearly had on the audience.

As has been said, Jesuit drama drew on a wide range of subject matter. The Bible was a favourite source of material, and the stories of Judith and Holofernes, Susanna, Tobias, Esther, the prodigal son, the wedding at Cana, the raising of Lazarus, to name but a few, were regularly dramatised. Other plays drew on history, both ancient and recent, and portrayed the lives of Alexander the Great, Xerxes, Sennacherib, King Herod, Constantine the Great, Julian the Apostate, Charlemagne, St Wenceslaus, Edward the Confessor, Alfonso the Learned of Castile, Emperor Charles V and Mary, Queen of Scots. Countless saints and martyrs, from Ambrose to Aquinas, Bernard of Clairvaux to Thomas-a-Becket, the Spanish martyr Eulalia to the Japanese martyrs of the first half of the seventeenth century, were commemorated in plays performed all over Europe. A favourite theme, dramatised by the Polish Jesuit Cnapius in 1597 and by the French Jesuit Caussin in 1620, was the story of St Felicitas, a pious lady martyred towards the end of the second century under the Emperor Antoninus. Rather than sacrifice to the pagan gods Felicitas is prepared to endure death. She has first to witness the cruel deaths of her seven sons, blazing the Christian trail to eternity before her eyes, before she herself after unspeakable tortures gains the martyr's crown. The details of her death and that of her sons are not glossed over by the dramatists and the Jesuit audience, for whom of course martyrdom was a very real possibility that had to be faced, will have been suitably uplifted and impressed. An example of plays showing the rewards of Christian conduct involving the cult of the Virgin is the *Odostratocles* of Cnapius,[2] in which a sinful brigand is saved from the wiles of the devil and the threat of eternal damnation by the fact that each day he offers up a prayer to the Virgin, a theme reminiscent of Bidermann's play *Jacobus Usurarius*. Plays on biblical themes were written by Miguel Venegas, a leading Spanish Jesuit playwright. His *Saul Gelboaeus*, first performed at Coimbra in 1559, deals with Saul's bloody end on Mount Gilboa as a direct result of his pride and duplicity; *Ahabus*, first performed in Coimbra probably in 1561, is a dramatisation of the story of Ahab and Jezabel; and *Absalon*, performed at Coimbra in 1562, is a version of the well-known Old Testament story. Venegas' plays exemplify well the international character of the Jesuit theatre, for they met with success in such divers countries as Spain, France, Germany and the Netherlands.[3] Perhaps the most splendid occasion in the history of Jesuit drama was the performance in 1659 of *Pietas victrix*, a play written and produced by the Austrian Jesuit Avancini and staged with tremendous pomp and circumstance in Vienna before an audience of some 3000 nobles and commoners with the Emperor Leopold I at their head. The play, dealing ostensibly with the 'victorious piety' of Emperor Constantine the Great and his defeat of Maxentius, was intended not only as a glorification of the Catholic Church but also as a triumphant paean to the House of Hapsburg and its ruling monarch. All the resources of the baroque stage were exploited to the full—hidden choruses, columns of fire, aerial battles between the Hapsburg eagle and the dragon of hell, contests on land and sea against a background of thunder and lightning and involving the hosts of heaven and the underworld; a striking testimony to the glory of God and the absolute power of the Hapsburg empire, and an indication of the way Jesuit drama developed in the fifty years since the Munich audience had sat in horrified silence at the end of the 1609 performance of *Cenodoxus*.

Jacob Bidermann was born in 1578 in the village of Ehingen, about thirty miles south-west of Ulm. Not a great deal is known about his life.[4] When he was eight years old he went to the Jesuit college at Augsburg, and remained as a pupil there until 1594. The college at Augsburg enjoyed at that time a very high reputation and was particularly distinguished by the presence of two Jesuits, the famous classicist and grammarian Jacob Pontanus and the theologian and scholar Matthaeus Rader, Bidermann's teacher and life-long friend. On 23 February 1594, at the age of sixteen Bidermann entered the Society of Jesus at Dillingen. After spending his novitiate at the Jesuit retreat at Landsberg from 1594 to 1597 he studied for three years at the college at Ingolstadt, and then spent three years teaching Jesuit pupils at Augsburg. After another three years studying theology at Ingolstadt he moved in 1606 to Munich, there to teach the 'disciplinae humaniores' at the Jesuit college. After nearly ten years there he moved in 1615, or early 1616, to Dillingen, where he was first professor of philosophy and then professor of theology at the Jesuit-controlled university. From there, probably in 1622, he was called to Rome to be official theologian of the Society and censor of books. He died in Rome on 20 August 1639.

Although his pastoral and teaching duties as a Jesuit claimed most of his attention, Bidermann nevertheless found time to write a good deal of verse—epigrams, epistolary poems, hymns, a verse epic *Herodias*—which was published during his lifetime and deservedly proved extremely popular. In addition he wrote various works of a devotional and philosophical nature. He also wrote a novel *Utopia* (published 1640), which is highly readable and entertaining. All these works, including the plays, were written in Latin. The plays were not published until twenty-seven years after his death (*Ludi Theatrales*, 1666). The fact that they were published at all is remarkable enough, for Jesuit plays were normally written for a special occasion, were rarely performed more than once or twice, and were then hardly ever subsequently published. The fact that they were gathered together and printed so many years after he died is a tribute to the lasting impression Bidermann's plays made on his contemporaries.

These plays anticipate to an extraordinary extent the themes and conflicts of German baroque drama in the middle of the seventeenth century. The role of fortune and the illusory nature of worldly fame are depicted in *Belisarius*, the dramatisation of the rise and fall of Justinian's general; the dream of life and the spiritual reality behind it is treated in *Cosmarchia*; the theme of the actor who plays the role of Christian martyr, only to assume it in reality, is portrayed in *Philemon Martyr*; two other plays dealing with the martyrdom of St Cassian and St Adrian have not survived; the theme of judgement that involves the damnation of Cenodoxus is dealt with in a conciliatory way in *Jacobus Usurarius*, where the sinful money-lender is saved from damnation by the intercession of the Virgin Mary; the role of the statesman and religious ruler is dramatised in *Josephus*; and three plays are concerned with the theme of retreat from the world and the embracing of the hermit existence, namely, *Macarius Romanus*, *Josaphatus*, and *Joannes Calybita*, the last mentioned achieving an extraordinary success when it was performed in Munich in 1638. All these different attitudes to the human comedy, where men enact their roles of statesman, general, martyr, scholar and hermit in a world of illusion dominated by the whims of Fortune, are then seen against the background of eternity and the ultimate reckoning, according to which the human soul is either saved or damned for all eternity. *Cenodoxus* is the best known of Bidermann's plays; but the others, in particular *Cosmarchia*, *Philemon Martyr* and *Joannes Calybita*, achieve a standard of excellence that makes him arguably the greatest of neo-Latin dramatists and the most important figure in German drama before Andreas Gryphius.

Cenodoxus is a dramatisation of the legend of the Doctor of Paris, associated in popular tradition with the founding of the Order of Carthusians by St Bruno. According to this legend, which was hardly challenged until well into the seventeenth century, Bruno was the witness of a miraculous event in Paris in 1082. A celebrated doctor, famed both for his learning and his virtue, died. As his obsequies were about to commence, the corpse rose up on the bier and cried out 'By God's just judgement I stand accused'. The funeral was postponed until the following day, when again the corpse exclaimed 'By God's just judgement sentence has been passed on me'. Again the funeral was postponed until the third day, when the corpse once more cried out 'By God's just judgement I am condemned'. Shocked by what he had seen, Bruno, together with six companions, thereupon retreated to the wilderness to form a community of hermit monks. The legend does not record the name of the doctor nor the sins for which he was damned.

Bidermann dramatises this legend and brings it up to date by identifying the reason the doctor was damned. Taking his cue from St Paul's epistles, where the word 'Cenodoxia', 'vain-glory', occurs (Galatians 5, 26, Philippians 2, 3), Bidermann ascribes the downfall of Cenodoxus to his spiritual pride. The idea of making a single sin responsible for his downfall, a sin that is not so much an external fault as one located within the soul of the individual, is entirely Bidermann's invention and, within the context of his times, highly modern. This becomes clear when the literary background of the sixteenth century is briefly sketched.

The sixteenth century was a period of strife and propaganda fought out against the changing background conditioned by the Renaissance and the Reformation. Man's relationship to God and to religion underwent a change. The distance travelled may be measured by the gulf that separates the mediaeval Everyman from the modern Faust.

The story of Everyman, the sinner overtaken by death, summoned to account before God for his sins on earth, and saved by his twelfth-hour repentance and good works, is well-known. Plays on this theme were repeatedly performed during the sixteenth century, and though the sinner might variously be saved according to whether he had put his trust in Catholic good works or Protestant faith, the pattern is essentially the same. A man lives a sinful life; he is visited by Death and told he must die; he is given a brief respite to repent and mend his ways; he is struck down by Death's bolt; and according to his deeds is saved or damned. With this class of play Bidermann will have been familiar. He will also have been familiar with another type of play that was common in sixteenth-century Germany, with plays dealing with the Last Judgement. This popular mediaeval theme forms the subject of many sixteenth-century plays, which were staged with great pomp, particularly at Easter. In them Christ is depicted not so much as a god of love but as a stern judge, proceeding with impartial justice to punish the guilty and reward the virtuous. Scenes showing the torments of the damned in hell were common and were painted with a vivid and doubtless terrifying realism. The devil had ceased to be a mediaeval figure of fun.

Cenodoxus to some extent clearly mirrors these two types of play, and it would be right to say that Bidermann observes the late mediaeval tradition captured by such plays. Into the mediaeval framework he has, however, put ideas that are modern and reflect new trends that had begun to make themselves felt towards the close of the sixteenth century. These trends may be indicated by the enumeration of a few significant dates.

In 1582 *Theophilus* was produced in the Jesuit college at Munich, and during the course of the next few years various versions of this play were produced in other Jesuit colleges. In 1587 the first version of Gretser's *Udo* was produced in Ingolstadt, and a second version was performed there in 1598. In 1587 the first version of the Volksbuch dealing with the life of Dr Faustus was published. In 1592 or thereabouts Marlowe wrote his *Tragical History of Doctor Faustus*. In 1602, the year *Cenodoxus* was performed in Augsburg, Shakespeare may well have written *Hamlet*. These dates bear witness to the growing strain imposed on the individual in relation to society, as the optimism of the rising individualism of the Renaissance and the early Reformation gave way to an increasing pessimism by the close of the century, when the individual was under attack both by orthodox Lutheranism and by the militant Catholicism of the Counter-Reformation. Religious tensions increased, witches were burned, public exorcisms became common, superstition was rife. The battle between heaven and hell for the individual soul assumed an added reality and urgency. Little wonder that the devil scenes in *Cenodoxus* filled the audience with terror.

The story of Theophilus, the man who entered into a pact with the devil to satisfy his thwarted pride and ambition, became bishop of Adana, had a vision of the Virgin and repented, dying in grace, was a popular one on the Jesuit stage. Theophilus cooperates with the grace offered and repents in time. Udo, archbishop of Magdeburg, does not repent and is damned. Udo, a backward student who, thanks to the help of the Virgin, became learned and was made an archbishop, led at first a godly life, but then changed for the worse, gave himself over to vice, and, disregarding warnings from heaven, died in mortal sin and was damned. His appearance before Christ at the Judgement was witnessed in a vision by the chaplain of the cathedral at Magdeburg, whilst his reception in hell at the hands of the demons was seen in another vision by the chaplain Bruno. Gretser's play, a considerable work of art compressed into forty-four pages of Latin,[5] contains several features relevant to *Cenodoxus*. The fame of the hero; the perversion of grace for human ends; the refusal of a man to repent; the struggle of heaven and hell for the possession of a man's soul; the damnation of a man because of his stubborn persistence in guilt; and his despairing cry of 'aeternitas!' as he is dragged off to burn perpetually in hell—all these features link *Udo* with *Cenodoxus*. Udo, whose words of self-justification are applauded by Cupido and Genius Malus, Lust and Evil Genius, just as Cenodoxus is applauded by Self-Love, mirrors those adventurous individuals who strained at the ties imposed on them by the Church, and his fate implicitly condemns them. In one important respect, however, he differs from Cenodoxus. Udo knows he is sinning. Cenodoxus is so trapped in his pride and self-love that in the end he sins unconsciously and maintains to his final dying moment the pose of the pious, stoic Christian.

Cenodoxus is the drama of the individual without grace, caught in the web of his individuality, the tragedy of the unqualified assertion of man's identity and its consequences for his soul. Cenodoxus is eternally damned, and the reason for his damnation is his spiritual pride. In choosing pride as the reason for the downfall of Cenodoxus Bidermann was singling out a vice that had long been branded by Catholic theologians as a deadly sin. Early church thinkers had listed eight such sins as the capital sins against which a Christian had to be on his guard, and two of these eight were vain-glory ('cenodoxia') and pride.[6] When later the pattern of seven deadly sins was ultimately evolved, pride was listed as the main sin and the source of all others. Pride, vain-glory, hypocrisy, self-love—these are facets of the one vice to which Cenodoxus is prey. Bidermann picks on a sin that was frequently denounced in the Middle Ages; but he presents it in a very modern light, modern from the point of view of the time in which he was writing. In Cenodoxus the pride of the humanist scholar is attacked and also the self-sufficiency of the Renaissance individual, so absorbed in the narcissistic contemplation of the self and so eager to bask in the fame learning brings, that he is deaf to the promptings of his better self and unwilling humbly to subordinate his desires to the will of God. This absorption in the ego and the pride that goes with it, consciously or unconsciously reflected in countless utterances by scholarly humanists and men of the Renaissance, the thirst for knowledge and the desire for fame based on the things of this world, aroused alarm in both the Catholic and Protestant Churches, which then proceeded to curb the pretensions of the individual through the warning examples of Faust, Theophilus, Udo and Cenodoxus. For such individualism and the pride that went with it represented a challenge to the authority of the Church as well as jeopardising the ultimate fate of the individual soul. The problem is pinpointed in the decisive fifth scene of the fourth act, where the guardian angel invites Cenodoxus to gaze at the stars whilst Hypocrisy offers him fame, the discoveries of this world, and the immortality that his fame will bring (1505–1514). Cenodoxus, for all his occasional wavering, fights to the last to preserve his individuality, and his daemonic urge to do this makes him a prey to the praise of fools and flatterers, makes him ignore the most terrible warnings sent from heaven, nightmare visions of hell and the crippling onslaught of disease, and leads him to persist in this attitude on his death-bed, where he takes the sacraments in a state of mortal sin.

Cenodoxus, the man filled with pride and vain-glory, is full of self-love and hypocrisy. But it must be stressed that this is not conscious hypocrisy on his part. He is no Tartuffe. He is an unconscious hypocrite; and even when he appears to be consciously hypocritical, as in the Navegus scene (ii, vi), he is quite unaware that he is thereby sinning, just as the Pharisee in St Luke, chapter 18, is not aware of any fault in his conduct. He genuinely believes that he is leading a pious and holy life, and that his good works will bring him salvation. He chooses to devote his life to cultivating fame and the immortality it will bring (i, iii), a choice made by many of Bidermann's contemporaries, and his persistence in remaining faithful to this choice blinds him to the true state of affairs.

His virtue is his downfall. Hypocrisy, unleashing 'new follies' on the world, uses virtue as the instrument of sin (176–182)— 'teaching them virtue, I teach them how to sin'. Cenodoxus, the learned man, the scholar, deceives others, but he deceives himself as well. A sombre state of affairs, and one in keeping with the pessimistic view of the contemporary world that Bidermann expresses in the words of Guarinus in II, i.

Virtue and wisdom become suspect, appearance and reality are confused, and human knowledge is made to appear questionable. Like a refrain the words 'scio' and 'nescio', often ironically employed, occur throughout the play, revealing the blindness of men. 'Ignorant of wounds, though wounded everywhere' (1431) is how the guardian angel describes Cenodoxus. The modern reader may well sympathise with the unfortunate doctor, for the themes implicit in the play— the problem of reconciling religion with the development of modern knowledge, the problem of spiritual pride, of narcissism, the illusory nature of truth and knowledge, and the extent to which intellectual refinement vitiates action—are modern enough. Bidermann writes from the Christian standpoint. But if one were to remove the Christian standpoint, then the lot of man, a plaything of supernatural forces and unable to trust his own powers of cognition and action, would be almost hopeless, and the words spoken by Self-Love (780–787) would open up a vista of despair.

It is, however, misleading to look at *Cenodoxus* in this way. Quite apart from the fact that Bidermann's sympathies are clearly on the side of Bruno and not of Cenodoxus, it needs to be stressed that the fate which overtakes Cenodoxus does not occur without an element of volition on his part. In 1581 the conflict between the respective merits of free-will and grace broke out between the Jesuits and the Dominicans and raged for nearly forty years throughout the Catholic Church. The Jesuits, through their spokesman Molina, stressed the importance of free-will, whereby man freely cooperates with the grace offered him by God. Cenodoxus chooses a particular path—'this die I've cast' (240)—and, however blinded he may be by his own self-love and vain-glory, in the end it is he who decides between the blandishments of Hypocrisy and Self-Love and the warning advice of his guardian angel and Conscience. The agents of heaven, as the guardian angel makes quite clear in the fifth act, cannot force their advice on Cenodoxus. They can warn and terrify through dreams; but in the end it is man himself who chooses between the forces of heaven and hell.

It is also misleading, when speaking of *Cenodoxus*, to speak of tragedy. Tragedy is concerned with the problems and values of this world. A play built around Christian values is concerned with problems of salvation and damnation that are ultimately resolved beyond the grave, 'sub specie aeternitatis'. Viewed solely in human terms the case of Cenodoxus might conceivably be tragic. From the point of view of the ultimate judgement Cenodoxus is a miserable sinner who, having deliberately ignored the help of Christ and His angels, deserves the punishment meted out to him.

It is Cenodoxus' misfortune that he is a learned man and that his intellect bars the way to that naivety of faith that might have saved him. In another play by Bidermann, *Jacobus Usurarius*, a thoroughly unpleasant and sinful money-lender is ultimately saved because of a last-minute repentance and because he has for some time in the midst of his daily routine found time to say a prayer to the Virgin. His faith, close to superstition though it may be, is naive and unreflecting. No narcissistic intellectual activity impedes the operation of grace. And he is eventually saved. The contrast between the fate of Cenodoxus and Jacob the money-lender calls to mind the fate of the two characters in Tirso de Molina's *El condenado por desconfiado*, though there is more in this play than this single contrast. The hermit Paulo has chosen a life of austerity and religious devotion not out of a disinterested love of God but to ensure his own salvation, fear of hell being a neurotic obsession. He forgets that man needs not only the mercy of God to be saved, but also charity—love of God and of one's neighbour. Too self-centred to be capable of love, Paulo loses hope in God's mercy, falls into the sin of despair and is damned. In contrast to him the criminal Enrico, whose sins in Paulo's eyes must inevitably merit damnation, presumes too much on the redeeming mercy of God as he flaunts his crimes before the world; but hidden from sight is his devoted love for and care of his crippled father, and it is this virtue of charity that leads him in the end to the humility and repentance that ensures his salvation. That the hermit is damned and the criminal saved has often been thought harsh, but from a divine point of view the verdict is just. Forgiveness of sins, made possible by the genuine exercise, however humble, of faith, hope and charity, is excluded by a self-centred persistence in spiritual pride.

If *Cenodoxus* is directed against the sin of pride it also contains an implicit attack against the neo-stoicism which, due primarily to the works of Justus Lipsius, was gaining ground in Europe at the turn of the century. The genesis of *Cenodoxus* may be in part attributed to the *De Constantia* (1584) of Lipsius. Bidermann was introduced to the writings of Lipsius by his teacher Rader and at first praised him in extravagant terms, only to reject his teachings later. When Lipsius died in 1606 Bidermann wrote to Rader expressing deep regret for all the time he had spent on the 'errores' of Lipsius, studies which had caused him great mental distress.[7] Lipsius' teachings, embodied in *De Constantia* in the person of Langius, are attacked in the character of Cenodoxus.

Neo-stoicism, which arose towards the close of the sixteenth century in response to the needs of the increasingly troubled times, was an attempt to square the doctrine of Christianity with the teachings of Epictetus and Seneca. After being initially attracted to it Bidermann recoiled from it in horror. It embodied, he considered, the pride of man in seeking to work out his salvation independently of God. However praiseworthy it may have been in extolling the virtues of constancy and moderation, inward harmony and self-integration, and in seeing learning and the study of the arts as a means to this end, it was ultimately ascribing to man the ability to achieve these goals and leaving God out of account. The difference between Bidermann and Lipsius can be demonstrated by two quotations. Man, according to St Ignatius, was created 'to praise, do reverence to and serve God our Lord, and thereby to save his soul',[8] in other words, man's being should be directed God-wards, and love and praise of God should inform his existence and actions on earth. The aim of right conduct, according to Lipsius, is to follow and obey Right Reason, 'and to be subject thereunto is to have the soveraintie in al humane affaires'.[9] On the face of it this is an admirable enough sentiment. Catholic doctrine did not object to the following of Right Reason in 'human affairs' and was certainly not inclined to play down the importance of the role assigned to human reason. What Bidermann will have objected to in *De Constantia* is the way that God is rarely mentioned, and then only perfunctorily, and the clear implication that man, following his reason, can fashion out for himself an existence on earth without the help of God and without keeping constantly in mind the ultimate issues of salvation and damnation. Bidermann will have made a distinction between stoic constancy, humanistically based, and true Christian constancy, consisting in a blend of iron will and complete dependence on the loving care of God. He will have detected in *De Constantia* an element of humanistic self-sufficiency and the spiritual pride arising from this. And, following the Ignatian tradition of seeing things in terms of black and white, and sensitive to the tendency of the age to polarise choices of conduct into either/or situations, he will have seen the alternatives clearly defined as selfless obedience to God's will on the one hand and selfish reliance on human capabilities on the other hand. To some extent Bidermann was swimming against the tide, as neo-stoicism, blended with Christian resignation, gained ground under the impact of the horrors of the Thirty Years War. But the solution he propounds in the person of St Bruno anticipates to an uncanny extent the solution to the trials of this world put forward by Grimmelshausen in *Simplicissimus* (1668), the most famous German novel of the seventeenth century, where the hero finally discovers the only way he can save his soul and counter the snares of earthly existence is to quit the world and become a solitary hermit.

Cenodoxus is modelled in great part on the figure of Langius. When he enumerates his virtues (I, iii) his words are almost a parody of the sentiments of Langius, whose praise of virtue in *De Constantia* is echoed in Cenodoxus' 'How noble, sweet and pious to strive for glory through virtuous practices' (599–600). The stoic virtues and the self-assurance of the stoic are reflected in III, iv, where Self-Love lists the good qualities of Cenodoxus. Neo-stoicism is parodied and attacked in the most terrible way in the deathbed scenes of IV, i and IV, iii. The modest refusal to appear learned, whilst being conscious of having learning, the pious way in which all is left to the mercy of God, the overcoming of the torments of the flesh, the yearning for death as the gateway to life, the moralising on the power of virtue and on the benefits of a holy existence, the constancy that brings tears to the eyes of those who stand by his bed—this is the stoic's end. And whilst Cenodoxus is confident that he is saved, the spectator of the play realises that he is hopelessly doomed. Cenodoxus dies in the odour of sanctity. But appearances deceive, and the reality revealed to Bruno and the others at the end of the play is very different.

Selfless surrender to the will of God and retreat from the world is the course finally chosen by Bruno and his companions. This is the final climax of the play and it is throughout geared to this. The title hero may be Cenodoxus; but it is Bruno, with his scornful and triumphant rejection of earthly joys, who points the moral and it is his condemnation of the world that is the yardstick by which the actions of Cenodoxus are to be measured. The figure of the hermit appears frequently in Bidermann's works. Three plays, *Macarius Romanus*, *Joannes Calybita* and *Josaphatus*, have as their heroes men who abandon the world to become hermits; a hermit appears in the play *Cosmarchia*; and many of the *Epigrams* deal with the experiences of hermits. Flight from the world and devotion to God is the answer provided by Bidermann to the deceptiveness of appearances and the transitory and fleeting nature of worldly things, and to the inability of man to solve his spiritual problems by human means alone. Bruno, it must be remembered, does not know why Cenodoxus is damned. He admired Cenodoxus whilst he lived; and the fact of his damnation means that values by which Bruno set store can no longer be regarded by him as meaningful and reliable, since he is not to know that Cenodoxus practised them in pride and hypocrisy. The course adopted by Bruno reflects a disillusionment with life and a resolve to escape from the snares of this world, and this mood appears to have been shared by many others, if the popularity of hermit plays during the first half of the seventeenth century is anything to go by. Bidermann's hermits, however, are not weaklings, running away from a world they cannot face up to. They are in the main forceful characters, entering upon their stark existence with a note of triumph, and Bruno is no exception to this. The example of the hermit also served a practical purpose, for Bidermann, writing a play to be performed on the Jesuit stage by Jesuit pupils, will have been mindful of the propagandist importance of the ideal of abandoning worldly ties to serve God in a religious order.

Three features of *Cenodoxus* help in particular to make it the effective play it undoubtedly is. One of these is the tripartite structure of the play. *Cenodoxus* is the story of a man involved in sin and damnation. Heaven and hell fight for the possession of his soul right up to the last breath he draws, and even beyond that, before the judgement seat of God. This structure of the play, in which the action takes place on the three planes of heaven, hell and earth, is typical of the plays of Bidermann, as indeed it is typical of Jesuit plays in general. Marlowe's *Faustus* ends with Faustus being carried off shrieking to hell. Bidermann does not stop there. For him death is not the end of all things. Man's fate is not sealed until judgement is finally pronounced on him by Christ the judge. This world and the next are alike the scene of the battle between supernatural forces over the soul of man, a battle in which the deciding word is spoken by man himself, by virtue of his free will. The scenes switch from heaven to earth and from earth to hell, emphasising the different planes of existence and their interdependence, engendering a sense of antithesis and a feeling of urgency and movement. Heaven terrifies Cenodoxus with devilish visions, and he is beguiled by devils playing heavenly music. Although the outcome of the struggle is judged 'sub specie aeternitatis' it is in this world, with its deceptive appearances, that man makes his choice between heaven and hell, and for the characters in Bidermann's plays no neutrality is possible. Nor was it easy for the audience to remain neutral, for this three-dimensional theatre extended beyond the action on the stage to confront the spectators with the same choice that the characters had to face.

It is a choice that Jesuits were encouraged to make when they performed the *Spiritual Exercises* of St Ignatius. These Exercises, inspired by visions Ignatius had of the Blessed Virgin in the church at Manresa and owing something too to the *Imitatio Christi*, the *Vita Christi* of the Carthusian Ludolf of Saxony and the *Ejercitatorio dela vida espiritual* by García de Cisneros (1500), clearly influenced Bidermann in the writing of *Cenodoxus*. The *Exercises* paint a vivid picture of heaven and hell, their eternal enmity, and the very real existence of both. The devil in the *Exercises* has a kind of grandeur and power, and hell acquires a frightening reality, as can be seen from the fifth exercises of the first week:

> The first prelude, a composition, which is here to see with the eye of the imagination the length, breadth, and depth of hell.
>
> The second, to ask for what I want: it will be here to ask for an intimate sense of the pain that the damned suffer, so that, if through my faults I become forgetful of the love of the Eternal Lord, at least the fear of pains and penalties may be an aid to me not to give way to sin.
>
> The first point will be to see with the eye of the imagination those great fires, and those souls as it were in bodies of fire.
>
> The second, to hear with the ears lamentations, howlings, cries, blasphemies against Christ our Lord and against all His Saints.
>
> The third, with the sense of smell, to smell smoke, brimstone, refuse and rottenness.
>
> The fourth, to taste with the taste bitter things, as tears, sadness, and the worm of conscience.
>
> The fifth, to feel with the sense of touch how those fires do touch and burn souls.[10]

This graphic description of hell is then reinforced by the Meditation on Two Standards of the fourth day of the second week, the two standards being those of Christ and Lucifer. Man has to choose between one or the other. This choice, a matter of his free will, is rendered clearer by rules Ignatius draws up for examining one's conscience, for distinguishing between good and evil spirits, for recognising one's sins and abhorring them, and for following different modes of humility. The subtlety of the devil is stressed:

> It is the way of the evil angel, who transforms himself into an angel of light, to go in with the devout soul and come out with himself, that is to say, to bring in good and holy thoughts, conformable to the said just soul; and afterwards he gradually contrives to arrive at his own end, dragging on the soul to his secret machinations and perverse intentions.[11]

and the danger of the devil using good works and pride to promote evil is underlined. Life is seen in terms of a battle between the forces of good and evil, a battle that admits of no neutrality. The *Exercises*, essential reading for the study of any Jesuit author, are a conditioning factor as far as the spiritual climate, urgency and tension of *Cenodoxus* are concerned.

The second notable feature of *Cenodoxus* is Bidermann's use of allegorical figures. The agents of heaven and hell are actively concerned in influencing man's choice of good or evil, as is clear from passages in the New Testament (Hebrews, I, 14, Ephesians, VI, 11–12). The existence of supernatural beings is taken for granted as they play their part in the fight for man's soul. Bidermann uses the allegorical figures very skilfully. They are not abstract appendages to the action, but are directly interested in the action of the play and indeed instigate it. They are real characters in their own right, each owing allegiance to either heaven or hell, for there are no neutrals in the world of the supernatural. They externalise the action, representing qualities that their speech and dress will have made clear to the audience. They serve a didactic function, emphasising the theme and missionary aim of the play in a way easily intelligible to the audience. But they are also used to reveal an inner conflict in a character or to make clear to the spectator a side of the character of which he himself is not conscious. Self-Love is Cenodoxus' alter ego, invisible to other human characters in the play, and when Self-Love comments on his utterances and prompts them it is as if Cenodoxus were wrestling with an inner conflict. It is fascinating to see how Bidermann uses the characters of Hypocrisy, Self-Love and Conscience, so that with their supernatural allegiances they are focal points of the spiritual struggle, whilst at the same time they enable the spectator to have insight into the psychological conflict going on within Cenodoxus himself.

The third notable feature of *Cenodoxus* is Bidermann's use of comedy. The play is serious enough, dealing as it does with the theme of judgement and rejection of the world. Yet it starts with a comic scene, and the first two acts contain a great deal of comedy. These scenes are funny, and had the 1609 Munich audience roaring with mirth. But in addition to providing entertainment for the groundlings they also

soften up the audience, so that the impact of the serious outcome is by contrast all the greater. This is clear from the
order of scenes, where comic scenes precede serious scenes
and where the comedy of the opening scene leads via the
social criticism of the opening scene of the second act, the
warning nightmare of the third, and the approach of disease
and death of the fourth, to the descent to hell, the 'Höllen-
sturz', of the fifth and Bruno's retreat from the world in order
to save his soul. Furthermore, the comic scenes mirror the
serious themes of the play and comment indirectly on them.
The opening line of the opening scene, whilst apparently
referring to Mariscus, clearly also implies Cenodoxus.
Mariscus is a hypocrite, just as is Cenodoxus, the one caught
up in the world of the senses, the other a prey to flattery and
spiritual pride. Both go to great lengths to achieve ignoble
ends and both delude themselves in the process. Dama uses
the plague as a comic means of vengeance on Mariscus; but
the plague, the plague of pride, really does infest the house,
as Hypocrisy makes clear in the next scene 'Meis Cenodoxus
irretitus est pestibus' (189/190). Mariscus tells the time of
day by the state of his stomach, just as modern man, according to T. S. Eliot, measures out his existence by coffee spoons,
and by indicating criticism of such a material existence
Bidermann adds depth to a typically Plautine situation.
Comic effect is achieved by the play on the supposed insanity
of Mariscus in 1, iv. But this play with insanity, a recurring
motif in Bidermann's works, implies a quest for identity and a
preoccupation with the self that is a comic mirror-image of
the situation in which Cenodoxus finds himself—and who
can say that Cenodoxus is of sound mind? A splendid example of the interplay of comic and serious themes is shown
in the scenes in which the shipwrecked sailor Navegus
appears. Here elements of classical comedy are fused with
mediaeval allegory and allusions to the Bible, with Navegus
and Cenodoxus cast in the roles of the publican and the
pharisee. The hypocrisy of Cenodoxus is exposed, and when
the sailor finally ruminates 'How much it matters, who asks
what, and when!' (766) he expresses a sentiment the truth of
which Cenodoxus will ruefully experience in the fifth act.
Other comic scenes, those with the countryman and with the
carpet thief, similarly mirror the themes of the deceptive

nature of appearances and the illusoriness of fame. Comic and serious themes intermingle, the comedy prepares the way for the serious denouement, so that in this sense the play is indeed a 'Comico-Tragoedia', and the comedy, so effective on the stage, is given an ironical colouring within the three-dimensional structure of the play, when viewed against the background of eternity.

The way that Bidermann uses comedy gives a clue to the reasons for the continuing success of his play. For *Cenodoxus* is living theatre. It is dramatically effective, metaphysically profound and psychologically acute. It combines elements of the comedy of Plautus and Terence with features of the Christian morality, and deals with problems that were not only modern at the time Bidermann wrote the play but are also of direct relevance to our own times.

Cenodoxus is written in the six-foot iambic verse used by Plautus, Terence and Seneca. In the free way he handles his verse Bidermann approximates more to Plautus and Terence, though his occasional use of epigrammatic phrase and stoic sentiment may owe something to Seneca. There are many allusions to classical authors, as well as to the Latin Vulgate, and these would no doubt have been picked up by the audience of Jesuit pupils, whom he would have taught in the classroom. It may seem strange to modern readers that the play should be written in Latin, a dead language. But Bidermann's Latin, with its down-to-earth realism and epigrammatic conciseness, classical allusions and punning witticisms, is anything but dead. It is a living theatrical language, and was experienced by his contemporaries as such. It is, however, by no means easy to translate such a packed and condensed vehicle of expression. In this translation the authors have tried to communicate the atmosphere of the play, whilst remaining as faithful as possible to the Latin within the limits of English blank verse.

The stage on which *Cenodoxus* was produced represented a development midway between the static theatre of the Renaissance and the theatre of the second half of the seventeenth century, when all the features of the modern stage were already present in their essentials. Basically Bidermann's stage must have been divided into two. The front half of the stage will have been left clear, while the back half will have consisted of two separate but inter-connecting rooms, curtained off from the front half and connected to it by doors. Rapid changes of scenes will thus have been possible, though where exactly each scene in *Cenodoxus* takes place is not quite clear. Perhaps the plan devised by Rolf Tarot in his excellent edition of the play and reproduced here is the best. This is how it looks:

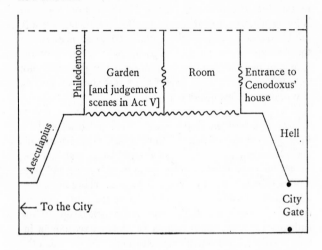

Cenodoxus was first published in the collected edition of Bidermann's plays, *Ludi Theatrales*, Munich 1666. There are two extant manuscripts of the play, both now in the Munich Staatsbibliothek. One, clm 8089, came from the Franciscan monastery of Kelheim and was copied down in 1610–11; the other, clm 11797, came from the Augustinian chapter at Polling, and dates from 1617–18. In 1635 a German translation of the play by Joachim Meichel was published in Munich. Both the manuscripts and the German translation differ in some respects from the printed version, which, if the preface to the 1666 edition is to be believed, is based on Bidermann's own revised text of the play. It is this 1666 version which is reprinted by Rolf Tarot in his edition, Max Niemeyer Verlag, Tübingen, 1963, and it is the Tarot edition that is reproduced here.

NOTES

1. The account of the 1609 Munich performance is contained in the preface, the *Praemonitio ad Lectorem*, of the edition of Bidermann's plays published in 1666 at Munich.

2. Gregorius Cnapius, *Tragoediae* (*Philopater, Faelicitas, Eutropius*), and *Odostratocles* have been edited by Professor Lidia Winniczuk and published in 1965 and 1969 respectively by the Polish Academy of Sciences. I am grateful to Professor Winniczuk for her help and cooperation.

3. Cf. Nigel Griffin, 'Miguel Venegas and the sixteenth-century Jesuit school drama', *Modern Language Review*, 68 (1973) 796–806.

4. The main source of information is Volume V of the *Historia Provinciae Germaniae Superioris*, the official history of the Jesuits in the Upper Province of Germany from 1541 to 1640. The fifth volume, written by Francis Xavier Kropf and published in 1754, covers the decade 1631–1640. A detailed account of Bidermann's life and career is included under the year 1639, the year of his death.

5. Gretser's play is contained in a manuscript in the Munich Staatsbibliothek, cod. lat. mon. 197572, fol. 785–829.

6. John Cassian (?360–430) lists *cenodoxia* and *superbia* as the seventh and eighth sins, Patrologia Latina, Vol. 49.

7. Bidermann's letters to Rader are contained in Cod. lat. mon. 1610, fol. 182–204. The undated letter from Ingolstadt concerning the death of Lipsius is on fol. 197ᵛ.

8. Quoted from the English translation of the Spiritual Exercises by Father Rickaby, S.J., London 1915, p. 18.

9. Quoted from the English translation by Sir John Stradling in 1594 reprinted by Rudolf Kirk, Rutgers University Press, New Brunswick 1939.

10. Rickaby, op. cit., pp. 40–1.

11. Rickaby, op. cit., pp. 143–4.

CENODOXUS *or, The Doctor of Paris*

COMICO-TRAGOEDIA

CENODOXUS, *the Doctor of Paris*
DAMA
LABEO } *servants to Cenodoxus*
NASO
MARISCUS, *a parasite*
AESCULAPIUS
MACHAON } *doctors*
PODALYRIUS
DORUS } *servants to*
DROMUS } *Aesculapius*
BRUNO, *a nobleman*
ANDREAS
GUARINUS } *noblemen,*
HUGO } *companions of*
LAUDWINUS } *Bruno*
STEPHANUS
PHILARETUS } *two noble*
PHILEDEMONES } *students*
NAVEGUS, *a shipwrecked sailor*
PTOCHUS } *two captives*
EXORISTUS
CLEPTES, *a thief*
RUSTICUS, *a peasant*
SMILAX } *two constables*
DROPAX
Funeral Chorus

CHRIST
ST MICHAEL } *and other members*
ST PETER } *of the heavenly*
ST PAUL } *tribunal*
CENODOXOPHYLAX,
    guardian angel to Cenodoxus
Chorus of Angels
PANURGUS
ASTEROTH } *devils*
ASEMPHOLOTH
PHASALLIOTH
Chorus of Devils
CONSCIENTIA, *Conscience*
HYPOCRISIS, *Hypocrisy*
PHILAUTIA, *Self-Love*
MORBUS, *Sickness*
MORS, *Death*
SPIRITUS CENODOXI,
    the Spirit of Cenodoxus

LECTORI, SPECTATORI.

Parisiaci Doctoris passim meminere multi: Nomen haud ullis
temere traditum. Iureconsultum alicubi legis; & magna
Eruditionis, nec nulla virtutis fama clarum: ut naturae concesserit, in feretro resedisse; indidem se Reum; altero post
die, Iudicatum; denique perennibus flammis addictum, pro-
clamasse: Ea de re Brunoni Carthusiensium Auctori primum
Auctorem fuisse, ut cum paucis alijs, & locum & vitam in
melius mutaret. Haec historia. Caeterum, quod illi Cenodoxo
nomen facimus, eiusque Superbiam vitiaque Superbiae
cognata notamus, fabula est. Quo enim crimine sit accusatus,
nobis in incerto habetur: quod inter flagitia propius fieri &
honestius repraesentari potuit, posuimus; Hominem
nulla insuper traductum calumnia cupimus.
Nam si talis illi vita fuit, convitium
haud fecimus: si non fuit, alius
vitam, huius mortem
memoramus.

TO THE READER, TO THE SPECTATOR.

The Doctor of Paris has frequently been made mention of by
many writers: but it so happens that none of them has
recorded his name. You will find it stated that he was a
lawyer; that he was famous and distinguished for his erudition and for his great virtue; and that when he paid his debt
to nature and died, he sat up on his bier, proclaiming that he
was accused; the following day that judgement had been
passed on him; and finally that he had been consigned to the
everlasting flames; because of this he was the primary inspira-
tion which inspired Bruno to found the Carthusian Order by
changing, together with a few kindred souls, his place of
habitation, and the tenor of his life, for the better. This much
history tells us. For the rest, our having given him the name
of Cenodoxus and imputed to him the sin of Pride and the
sins linked with Pride, is our own invention. We cannot state
with any certainty of which sin he was accused; and we have
chosen that sin which of all the sins could be most properly
and fittingly portrayed. It is no wish of ours to burden this man
with additional charges against his name. If his life was as
we have portrayed it, then the abuse he suffers
is not of our making: if it was not, then
what we are recounting is someone else's life and this
man's death.

ACTUS I

DAMA: Ut inferi inferaeque perdant noxium
Caput; usque nebulo ludit evertitque herum
Inanijs, affanijs, offucijs,
Mendacijs. Palpat, prehensat, aestimat,
Adulat, ambit, tollit illum ad Sidera, 5
Et si quid ultra sidera est. Piget, pudet
Audire toties. Cui rei autem haec factitat?
Ut coenulam ab hero eblandiatur: hinc dies
Nulla mihi abit, quin centies negotium
Facessat. Ostio accubat prope perdius 10
Pernoxque. Nunquam progredior ego, quin statim
Ad me ille; Dama, quid herus hodie? an est satis
Salve? occupatur etiam? an etiamnum vacat?
Jamne ille coenat? jamne alicubi inambulat?
Aiam ego, negemve, juxta habet: viam invenit 15
Qua sese in aedes penetret: & si me audiat
Paullum dicacem, in proximo est ut verberet.
Ulciscar hodie tenebrionem, & annuas
Injurias luet diali inedia.
Edixit enim heri, ad nos venire in prandium. 20
Nec differet, cum noverit adesse hospites.
Sed ludio ludetur. Equidem jam mihi
Hanc fabulam dictavi. At eccum, hic ipsus est
Ipsissimus, qui prodit. Ego nunc me apparo.
MARISCUS: Caelum errat indubie, meroque plusculum 25
Sol potus hodie se fefellit. Nam mihi
Liquidum est, meridiem adesse: quicquid clamitent

Act One

DAMA: Infernal gods! Destroy this baneful man
    Who plays upon my master with such lies,
    Inanities, deceits and idiocies.
    He wheedles, toadies, flatters, fawns, crawls, drools,
    Praising him to the skies and far above,
    (That's if there's anything above the skies!).
    I'm sick with shame to hear this all the time.
    Why does he do it? Just to worm some meal
    Out of my master. Not a day goes by
    Without a hundred of these ploys. He's here
    Propping our doorpost morning, noon and night.
    I can't go out without him starting up:
    'Your master, Dama, how is he today?
    Is he quite well? Or busy? Is he free?
    Eating? Or walking?' If I say yes or no
    It's all the same: he soon finds some way in.
    And if he hears me make a crack at him
    He lashes out. But here's my day of vengeance
    For a year's insults: he'll get no food today.
    He told us yesterday he'd come for lunch.
    He won't be late–he knows we're having guests.
    I'll trick the trickster. I've a story ready
    That I've rehearsed. But here's the man himself,
    His very self, arriving. I'll get ready.
MARISCUS: Undoubtedly the sky's off course today,
    The sun's got drunk and muddled. For to me
    It's crystal clear that noon's upon us now,

Sonora turrium aera; certior meas
Mihi vigil aures vellicat: is, ubi surgere
Cubitu jubet, certum est mihi, esse septimam: 30
Idemque rursus quando prandere imperat,
Meridiem; ubi coenare suadet, vesperam;
Saturum ubi me esse dicit, est crepusculum.
Jam, quicquid umbra mentiatur, prandium
Ait imminere: quod has ego apud aedes modo   35
Inhiabo; nam hic Cenodoxus incolit meus;
Qui quantum abhorret ab alijs, tantum mihi
Inhaeret. At neque joculares illi ego
Nugas, neque hoc genus alios verniliter
Divendo risus, ut aliqui nunc assolent;   40
Sed grandibus demulceo illum laudibus,
Caeloque adaequo. Dignus an sit, haud scio;
Sed mihi, ita dicere, utile esse, istuc scio.
At cesso adire! Aperite aliquis hoc ostium.
Aperite. Nemone hodie ad has curat fores?   45
Aperite.

DAMA: Quid clamoris hic? quid est rei?
MARISCUS: Aperite confestim: aut viam vi ego facio.
DAMA: Facesse, moneo: aut?
MARISCUS: Quid tuum hoc, aut?
DAMA: Aut caput
          Lapide hoc repente elido.
MARISCUS: Scelus, etiam has minas?
          Aperite, moneo.   50
DAMA: Abscede, moneo; aut denuo.
MARISCUS: Nae tu es mihi imperiosus his in aedibus!
DAMA: Nam sunt meae: haud patiar, molestus ut sies.
MARISCUS: Tun' ergo, flagrio, dicis has aedes tuas?
DAMA: Quippini enim? an has fortasse non custodio?
MARISCUS: Ut ne quis illas nempe secum hinc auferat?   55
DAMA: Imo ut ego te hinc in maximam malam crucem
          Recta auferam. Sed cedo, quid est negotij
          Tibi has ad aedes, hoc diei, hoc temporis?
MARISCUS: Rogas, tenebrio? ubi Cenodoxus est modo?
DAMA: Cenodoxus?   60
MARISCUS: Ipse hic, inquio.
DAMA: Ille qui hanc domum
          Heri incolebat?

Whatever noise the bell-tower chimes boom out.
My inner clock's more accurate: for when
It tells me to get up, I know it's seven;
Then when it orders lunch, I know it's noon;
It's evening, clearly, when it orders dinner;
Twilight, when it admits that I'm quite full.
So now, whatever shady lies the sky tells,
'Lunch is imminent!' my clock says. Here,
At this house, I'll gape upon it open-mouthed.
For here resides my dear friend Cenodoxus,
Who clings the more to me the more he shies
From everybody else. I don't, like others,
Make trifling jests, offer him servile jokes.
No, I caress him with grand words of praise,
Exalt him to the skies. Whether he's worthy of it
I hardly know, but I *do* know he's worth it!
But here I am! Arrived! Open this door up!
Open, I say! Is no-one on the door?
Open!

DAMA: Why, what's this noise? And what's the matter?

MARISCUS: Open up sharp or else I'll force my way.

DAMA: Clear off, or else....

MARISCUS: What do you mean, or else?

DAMA: Or else I'll bash your head in with this stone.

MARISCUS: You rascal, do you dare to threaten me?
        Open, I say!

DAMA: And you clear off, I say.

MARISCUS: You order me about and boss the house!

DAMA: Why not? It's mine. I'll have no trouble from you.

MARISCUS: You scoundrel you, you say this house is yours?

DAMA: Indeed it is. Don't I watch over it?

MARISCUS: So nobody walks off with it, no doubt?

DAMA: So I can see you cop it good and proper,
        A noose around your neck. But what's your business?
        What brings you to this house this time of day?

MARISCUS: You dare to ask, you wretch? Where's Cenodoxus?

DAMA: Cenodoxus?

MARISCUS: Yes.

DAMA: The man who yesterday
        Lived in this house?

MARISCUS: Hic ipse.

DAMA: Ille, qui fores
    Commisit has mihi?

MARISCUS: Nempe hic ipse: quid rogas?

DAMA: Ille qui herus est meus?

MARISCUS: Ipse: quaeso te an sapis?

DAMA: Ille, his qui abesse te aedibus suis jubet?

MARISCUS: Ille, ille, scelus, ille, ille; qui te in furcam agat,   65
    Trifurcifer. Potin' ut mihi respondeas,
    Cenodoxus ubi sit?

DAMA: Est ibi, ubi sese esse vult;
    Et ubi esse te nevult.

MARISCUS: Puer, ego ni tibi
    Magnum malum dedero, Marisco dent alij.

DAMA: Quid video? tun' eras, Marisce? ita me meus   70
    Herus amet, ut ego alium esse rebar. Quin mane,
    Aperio.

MARISCUS: Nolo. Puerum ego hunc, ubi primulum
    Cenodoxon adiero, ulmeum totum dabo:
    Ita vindicabo.

DAMA: Mane, mane; non noveram.

MARISCUS: Quem me ergo, stulte existimabas?   75

DAMA: Futilem
    Homuncionem aliquem, stolonem, stipitem,
    Bardum, stuporem, vappam.

MARISCUS: Itane caecutias
    Meridie?

DAMA: Ita est. Sed an ego jam hic te quaererem
    Marisce? quem jam in prandio esse oportuit.

MARISCUS: Essem, nisi hic esses. An igitur jam licet   80
    Tandem ingredi?

DAMA: Quonam?

MARISCUS: Huc?

DAMA: Licet tibi; dummodo
    Ne terreare.

MARISCUS: Quidum enim?

DAMA: Circumspice,
    Ne quis sit arbiter.

MARISCUS: Quid est?

DAMA: Circumspice,
    Inquam, an quis audiat?

MARISCUS: Yes, yes.
DAMA: Who made me watchman
    To guard this door?
MARISCUS: Of course. Why ask me that?
DAMA: My master?
MARISCUS: Yes! Have you gone raving mad?
DAMA: The man who sees you off these premises?
MARISCUS: Yes, that one, that one, scoundrel. He'll make sure
    Your goose is cooked. Why can't you answer me?
    Where's Cenodoxus?
DAMA: Where he wants to be;
    And where he wants you not to be.
MARISCUS: If I don't beat you,
    And beat you hard, let others beat Mariscus.
DAMA: What, *you* Mariscus? Why, I'll stake my wages
    I really thought that it was someone else.
    I'll open up.
MARISCUS: I won't put up with it.
    I'll thrash that slave at one word from his master.
    I'll pay him back.
DAMA: Wait, wait: I didn't know you.
MARISCUS: Who did you think I was, you fool?
DAMA: Some idle
    Nincompoop, some useless clod or growth,
    Some vapid, addled, good-for-nothing oaf.
MARISCUS: So blind at noon?
DAMA: Why, how could I expect
    You here, Mariscus, when you should be lunching?
MARISCUS: If you weren't here I would be. May I please
    Come in at last?
DAMA: Where?
MARISCUS: Here!
DAMA: So long as you're
    Not frightened.
MARISCUS: Why on earth?
DAMA: Look round in case
    We're being watched.
MARISCUS: Whatever for?
DAMA: Look round,
    Make sure there's no-one listening.

MARISCUS: Loquere, soli sumus.

DAMA: Nostine Bromium nostrum?   85

MARISCUS: Herilem scilicet
    Coquum?

DAMA: Hunc ajo: gibbosum illum, & hominem luridum.

MARISCUS: Teneo.

DAMA: Ille, cum hodie ad prandium jam pleraque
    Parasset; at, quaeso te, adhuc circumspice.

MARISCUS: Quin pergis?

DAMA: Ante focum repente concidit.

MARISCUS: Concidit?   90

DAMA: Ita, inquam; & miseriter, prae quam putes,
    Exclamat. Accurrimus: ait, se biduum
    In peste jam cubare.

MARISCUS: Quid? peste?

DAMA: Obsecro
    Marisce, porge manum; ita adhuc nimio metu
    Percellor, ubi recordor.

MARISCUS: Abstine hinc manum.

DAMA: Quid refugis?   95

MARISCUS: Abstine.

DAMA: Quid est modo?

MARISCUS: Abstine.

DAMA: Non audies reliquum?

MARISCUS: Audiam, si tu eminus
    Loquaris.

DAMA: At mallem aliqua in aurem dicere.

MARISCUS: Abscede: in auram loquere, Dama; minus erit
    Periculi.

DAMA: Igitur herus profugit cum suis,
    Meque hic reliquit, cum atriensi servulo,   100
    Ut esset aedium interim custodia.

MARISCUS: Et quo recessit, inquis, herus? inde loquere,
    Ne accede.

DAMA: Nosti, ubi in suburbano suos
    Hortos habeat herus? ibi te ille in prandium
    Expectat.   105

MARISCUS: Ubi? monstra obsecro.

DAMA: Vin' me ducem!

MARISCUS: Absiste, nolo. Caeterum eminus mihi
    Ostende, qua nam commeandum illuc siet!

MARISCUS: Speak up. We're all alone.

DAMA: Did you know Bromius?

MARISCUS: The master's cook?

DAMA: The very man. A hunch-backed, sallow chap.

MARISCUS: That's him.

DAMA: Well, while he was preparing things
    For lunch today – but just look round again.

MARISCUS: Get on with it.

DAMA: He suddenly collapsed right by the stove.

MARISCUS: Collapsed?

DAMA: That's what I said. And groaned more horribly
    Than you can think – told us, as we rushed up,
    He'd had the plague two days.

MARISCUS: What's that? The plague!

DAMA: Give me your hand, Mariscus. Just the thought
    Quite scares me stiff.

MARISCUS: You keep your hand away.

DAMA: Why back away?

MARISCUS: Keep off!

DAMA: What's up?

MARISCUS: Keep back!

DAMA: Why, won't you hear the rest?

MARISCUS: Yes, – from a distance.
    Go on.

DAMA: I'd rather say it in your ear.

MARISCUS: Get back: it won't be quite so dangerous, Dama,
    To say it to the air.

DAMA: Master and all
    Have left me here with just the steward's lad,
    To guard the house as long as they're away.

MARISCUS: So where's the master gone? Tell me from there, –
    No! Don't come any nearer!

DAMA: You know the suburb
    Where master has his gardens? He's expecting you
    To lunch there.

MARISCUS: Where? Please tell me.

DAMA: Come, I'll take you.

MARISCUS: No! Keep away! Just tell me from a distance
    Exactly how I have to find my way.

DAMA: Primum ergo turrim proximam transi; dein
　　　Sinistra porticus patebit, hanc cave
　　　Ne dexter ineas: laevus inde in angulum　　　　　　110
　　　Deflecte; post paullum regredere ad dexteram,
　　　Tum rursus ad sinistram, & iterum ad dexteram;
　　　Ibi videbis.
MARISCUS:　　　Quid ? suburbanum ?
DAMA:　　　　　　　　　　　　Nihil;
　　　Expecta; ibi civem videbis quempiam
　　　Hoplitodromum Megaloperiphronesterum,　　　　　115
　　　Qui venit illuc ex Pyrgopolitoxia.
MARISCUS: Hoplitodromum, Megaloperiphronesterum.
　　　Hui quale nomen ? Ego quidem antelucio
　　　Si prima ab eius littera ire incepero,
　　　Nox sit, prius quam ad ultimam pervenero.　　　　120
DAMA: Proin, facem sumas tibi & viaticum;
　　　Pronunciare cum cupis. Sed ita est: abi.
MARISCUS: Ibi Cenodoxum habebo ?
DAMA:　　　　　　　　　　Nihil: ibi poteris
　　　Requirere. Tenes ?
MARISCUS:　　　　　　Haud satis; at est tandem opus
　　　Tenere, nisi malim esurire. Modo abeo　　　　　　125
　　　Cenodoxon indagare. Male fecit mala
　　　Haec pestis; illum ejecit aedibus; mihi
　　　Injecit esuritionem.
DAMA:　　　　　　Abijt lues
　　　Herilis. Ego scio herum intus esse; atque cupide
　　　Hanc belluam expectare; eaque gratia　　　　　　130
　　　Mihi imperasse, uti vocarem. Ego Cretice
　　　Jam mentiar, vidisse nusquam; haud anxius
　　　Quo abeat Mariscus. Nec dubito quin vapulem,
　　　Si haec dixerit: Sed huius ego non fecero,
　　　Obduruit jam ad flagra tergus. Volupia est,　　　　135
　　　Si impransus hodie sit Mariscus. Ego velim
　　　Vel coenula carere etiam, ut ipse careat.

DAMA: Walk past the tower, the one right here, and then
          You'll see an arcade on your left—walk in it,
          Not to the right, though; bear then to the left,
          Around a corner; take the next turn right,
          Go left soon after, then turn right again.
          Before your eyes...

MARISCUS: I'll see the suburb gardens?

DAMA: No, no, just wait. You'll see a man who's called
          Hoplitodromus Megaloperiphronesterus,
          Come all the way from Pyrgopolitoxia.

MARISCUS: Hoplitodromus, Megaloperiphronesterus!
          What sort of name's this? If I start at dawn
          And move on from one letter to the next,
          It'll be dark before I've reached the last.

DAMA: Well, if you want to spell it out exactly,
          Take money and a torch, and off you go!

MARISCUS: Where I'll find Cenodoxus?

DAMA: No! That's where
          You ask again. Right?

MARISCUS: Right it has to be,
          Unless I want to starve. So off I go
          To look for Cenodoxus. Pestilence
          Take this foul plague. It's rid the house of him,
          And riddled me with hunger.

DAMA: Off goes *that* plague—
          My master's friend! I know he's there inside,
          Waiting this monster's coming eagerly.
          That's why he told me to invite him in.
          I'll swear I never saw him. I don't care
          How far Mariscus strays. No doubt I'll suffer
          A beating if he tells. Well, never mind,
          My back's inured to blows. And what pure pleasure
          If that Mariscus misses lunch today.
          I'll gladly starve myself, if he does too.

SCENA II
HYPOCRISIS, PANURGUS,
ASTEROTH, ASEMPHOLOTH

HYPOCRISIS: Relinquo tetros orbis inferi specus,
　　　Noctisque caecos per recessus, aetherem
　　　Reviso superum: ne sit uspiam meis　　　　　　　　140
　　　Intacta damnis plaga. Venite, currite,
　　　Huc huc Averno socia properate agmina,
　　　Audite, adeste.
PANURGUS:　　　　　Hui, quis ruentes evocat
　　　Acherunte turmas?
ASTEROTH:　　　　　　　Ecquis ausus inferis
　　　Dare jura regnis?　　　　　　　　　　　　　　145
ASEMPHOLOTH:　　　Cuius imperio meas
　　　Relinquo sedes?
HYPOCRISIS:　　　　Ego citavi, Hypocrisis:
　　　Adeste; vel consulere vos, vel prodere
　　　Vobis placet consulta.
PANURGUS:　　　　　　Prode; seu dolo
　　　Nostro indiges, sive manu; in utrumque adsumus
　　　Dudum apparati: prode.　　　　　　　　　　　150
HYPOCRISIS:　　　　　Molior novas
　　　Foecunda scelerum mater orbi insanias,
　　　Vulneraque meditor, quae nec hasta Pelias
　　　Quidem levassit.
OMNES:　　　　　Adjuvamus.
HYPOCRISIS:　　　　　　　Perditis
　　　Imo mea coepta, improvidi, nisi facitis
　　　Nunc imperanda.　　　　　　　　　　　　155
OMNES:　　　　　Facimus; impera, impera.
HYPOCRISIS: Philautiam mihi comitem date; caeteras
　　　Orci sorores inquio, Tyrannida,
　　　Furiasque Saevitiemque abire cogite.
PANURGUS: Quae culpa?
HYPOCRISIS:　　　　　Turbant atque terrent. Blandior
　　　Plures ego ambio. Nimis enim jam artibus　　　160
　　　Pugnant Furiae apertis; vetusta saecula
　　　Decipere doctae; cum parentum adhuc gulas
　　　Jugulosque fratrum, Conjugumque sanguinem
　　　Haurire licuit; cum impianda noxias

SCENE II
HYPOCRISY, PANURGUS,
ASTEROTH, ASEMPHOLOTH

HYPOCRISY: I leave the underworld's foul cavernous depths,
　　　Night's dark recesses to traverse again,
　　　Revisiting the upper air, where nothing
　　　Escapes my blighting harm. You allied throngs
　　　From dark Avernus, hasten here, come, run,
　　　Hasten and hear.
PANURGUS:　　　Who summons forth the swarms,
　　　The hosts of Acheron?
ASTEROTH:　　　　Who dares to lord it
　　　Over the infernal realms?
ASEMPHOLOTH:　　　　And at whose bidding
　　　Do I leave my realm?
HYPOCRISY:　　　　I summoned you, Hypocrisy.
　　　Come, gather round, hear my advice, or else
　　　Advise me.
PANURGUS:　　Tell us your plans. And if you need
　　　Our cunning or our strength, both are long ready.
　　　Now speak.
HYPOCRISY:　　Fertile begetter of evil deeds
　　　I toil to unleash new follies on the world
　　　And conjure wounds that even Achilles' spear
　　　From Pelion could not alleviate.
ALL:　　　　　　We'll aid you.
HYPOCRISY: Your improvidence will ruin my designs
　　　Unless you do my bidding.
ALL:　　　　　　We will; command us.
HYPOCRISY: Give me Self-Love, then, to be my companion;
　　　And compel the other hellish sisters all–
　　　Tyranny, the Furies, Cruelty–to go.
PANURGUS: Why?
HYPOCRISY:　　　Fear and confusion are their tools, while I
　　　Soothe and entice more subtly. For too long
　　　The Furies have waged open war; past ages
　　　They had the skill to ensnare, when parents' throats
　　　And brothers' veins were slit, and blood of wives
　　　Could be consumed; and guilty Thebes was steeped

Fecere Thebas scelera: tunc Furijs honos   165
Erat aliquis. Sed alia nunc tempora, alij
Mores, alij homines volunt scelerum alios
Duces.

OMNES: Bene, callide.

ASEMPHOLOTH: Quis ille vero criminum
Auctor?

HYPOCRISIS: Magistra ego talis, ac dux prodeo
Generata tetrae noctis in sinu Hypocrisis,   170
Quae, quotquot Acheruns parturit strophas, lues,
Cladesque perniciesque pestesque, unica
Triumpho cunctas. Nulla quo pervadere
Vis Stygia potuit, Hypocrisis ego potui.
Compendio, quae & quanta sim, dicam. Mihi   175
Vel ipsa virtus addit incrementa; me
Nutrit suo alimento; evehit, fovet sinu.
Recteque facta ego suadeo, doceo, approbo,
Invito, perpello, urgeo, traho, rapio
Probitatis ad fastigium; at quo ego propius   180
Adduco, tanto abducere soleo longius.
Peccare doceo, dum doceo bene vivere.
Virtutem amando, odi; fovendo, interneco.
Nec praeda me quaevis juvat: animos lego
Non infima de plebe: praecipui abeunt   185
Plerumque praecipites. Neque illos vivere
Bene, veto; dum ita vivant bene, ut mori male
Possint.

OMNES: Tibi omnes cedimus, quotquot sumus.

HYPOCRISIS: Id est, quod hoc loci quoque studeo. Meis
Cenodoxus irretitus est pestibus: Habet.   190

OMNES: Quae praeda?

HYPOCRISIS: Lauta, clara, opima, splendida.
Ille Cenodoxus, inquio, nova gloria
Sidusque Doctorum fori Parisiaci.

PANURGUS: Quid enim actitat?

HYPOCRISIS: Quicquid jubere ego soleo.
Tumet, sibique perplacet: quaerit bonus   195
Videri.

PANURGUS: At esse?

HYPOCRISIS: Nihil habet pensi: Probum
Turba facit; ubi abit arbiter, virtus abit.

In crimes inexpiable; some honour then
The Furies gained. But now the times are changed:
Other customs, other men, seek other
Spurs to crime.

ALL:　　　　　　　　Well said, and shrewdly said.

ASEMPHOLOTH: Who, then, leads their crimes?

HYPOCRISY:　　　　　　　　　　　I am their mentor:
Born of baneful night, Hypocrisy,
I lead, sole general, in my triumph all
The agues, plagues, disasters, stratagems
That Hell has given birth to. Where no might
Of Styx can penetrate, I find a way.
The nature of my powers is briefly put:
Virtue itself increases them, it fattens me
On its own food, suckles me at its breast.
I urge to righteous actions, teach, encourage,
Persuade, propel, spur on, draw, force
To heights of probity; and make men fall
To baser depths, the higher I make them climb.
Teaching them virtue, I teach them how to sin.
Kill it by cherishing, by loving hate it.
Not every prey delights me: I choose souls
Not from the lowest class, but from the highest—
Their fall's the further. Nor do I bid them live
Unrighteously, if through their virtuous life
They die in sin.

ALL:　　　　　　　　We give you pride of place.

HYPOCRISY: Such then is my design: my baneful wiles
One Cenodoxus have ensnared. He's mine.

ALL: What prey is this?

HYPOCRISY:　　　　　　A famous, splendid one,
Ripe to be plucked; the star and latest glory
Of all the Paris doctors—Cenodoxus.

PANURGUS: What does he do?

HYPOCRISY:　　　　　　　Whatever I bid him do.
Puffed up with pride and love of self, his aim
Is to seem good.

PANURGUS:　　　　And is he?

HYPOCRISY:　　　　　　　　No. His virtue
Needs an audience; unregarded, it disintegrates.

    Simulare, dissimulare, fingere, tegere,
    Jactare sua, temnere aliena; Neminem
    Suspicere, suspici ab omnibus: livescere   200
    Gloria aliena, insurgere sua, non parem,
    Non ferre proxime sequentem, ita callide
    Tenere Cenodoxus didicit, uti queat
    Vel me docere: quodque caput est, Nemini,
    Neque adeo sibi suspectus est.   205
PANURGUS: Sat dixti. Habet.
HYPOCRISIS: Abite, si probatis.
OMNES: Imus, qua voles.
    Jube, impera, praecipe.
HYPOCRISIS: Modo ite, dum vocem.
    Ruina nunc, & finis apparandus est
    Mihi. Caeterum, nisi ego animi fallor, dabo,
    Dabo peractam hanc fabulam. Ite; ego hac eo.   210

SCENA III
CENODOXUS, PHILAUTIA

CENODOXUS: Alios quiescere cura non sinit; alios
    Adversa fors. Mihi secunda parturit
    Aura inquietem. Gratiae ac Faventiae
    Videntur omnes insidere pectori
    Meo. Favore, honoreque premor undique.   215
PHILAUTIA: Mereris. Haec virtutibus merces venit.
CENODOXUS: Quacunque pergo, in me sua omnis lumina
    Obvertit aetas.
PHILAUTIA: Imo virtutem in tuam.
CENODOXUS: Monstrare me digito solent: Hic ne, inquiunt,
    Est ille Cenodoxus, quem adorat civitas?   220
PHILAUTIA: Non sola civitas, sed orbis.
CENODOXUS: Ille, quem
    Hodie eruditorum facile primum putant?
PHILAUTIA: Id non putant; sciunt.
CENODOXUS: Quem adiri ab omnibus
    Constat, quibus consilia, spem, remque petere est
    Necesse?   225
PHILAUTIA: Nempe omnia tu es unus omnibus.
CENODOXUS: Quem tanta probitas, tanta sanctimonia
    Cohonestat?

    Pretence, dissimulation and deceit,
    Vainglory, scorn of others; honouring none
    Above him, honoured by all; sickened with envy
    At others' fame, full of his own, intolerant
    Of equals or near-equals; in such skills
    Is Cenodoxus so conversant, I
    Could be his pupil; and to crown it all
    No-one, least of all himself, suspects him.

PANURGUS: Enough. He's done for.

HYPOCRISY: Go then.

ALL: As you wish.
    Give us your orders.

HYPOCRISY: Go, await my call.
    His ruin and his end must be prepared
    By me. I'll give the finish to this play
    Of his, unless I'm much mistaken. Go!

SCENE III

CENODOXUS, SELF-LOVE

CENODOXUS: To some, anxiety allows no calm, to others
    Adverse fate. I'm not becalmed, for favourable
    Are the winds that waft me. All the Graces seem
    To occupy my breast. And favours, honours,
    Crowd in upon me from all sides.

SELF-LOVE: Deservedly
    To virtues such as yours come such rewards.

CENODOXUS: Go where I may, the eyes of all the age
    Are turned on me.

SELF-LOVE: And gaze upon your virtue.

CENODOXUS: They point me out saying 'Isn't that the man,
    That Cenodoxus whom the state reveres?'

SELF-LOVE: Not just the state, the world.

CENODOXUS: The man, they think,
    Of all the learned men by far the first?

SELF-LOVE: Not merely think, they know.

CENODOXUS: To whom all go
    Who need to seek advice, or hope, or help?

SELF-LOVE: For you alone are all things to all men.

CENODOXUS: Whom such great probity and sanctity
    Combine to honour?

PHILAUTIA: Imo qui ipse Sanctimoniam
    Honestat.
CENODOXUS: Illud Gallici lumen soli?
PHILAUTIA: Sol ipse.
CENODOXUS: Regis animus?
PHILAUTIA: Et Regni salus.
CENODOXUS: Haec dictitant, aliaque, quibus ego ut habear   230
    Dignus, nihil laboris est, quod denegem.
PHILAUTIA: Bellum est, videri; & comparandum quolibet
    Pretio.
CENODOXUS: Mihi etenim a vigilijs, insomnijs,
    Studiisque noctes ac dies paene pereunt.
PHILAUTIA: Perire non potest, quod hominum laudibus   235
    Perennat.
CENODOXUS: Atqui, quantulis laboribus
    Quantos honores est apisci? Vivere
    Id esse demum censeo, contendere,
    Ut me emori facinora clara non sinant.
    Haec alea mihi est jacta.   240
PHILAUTIA: Non, etsi velis,
    Dehinc latere poteris: insita est tibi
    Virtus; coli debet; velis, nolis coli.
CENODOXUS: Aeterne Rector orbis! Unde ego gratias
    Tibi habebo dignas, quando me his virtutibus
    Ornas, ut invideant mihi omnes, nulli ego?   245
PHILAUTIA: Fortuna digna hoc animo; & ista dignus est
    Fortuna animus.
CENODOXUS: Et vero me tenues opum
    Adeunt vicem parentis, obsecrant, colunt,
    Me praedicant, amantque. Sublevo meis
    Illorum inopiam opibus: Rogari adeo stipem   250
    Non sustineo; sed occupare fere solet
    Munifica dextra, precemque stips praevertere.
PHILAUTIA: Ipsa Pietas palmam tibi concesserit.
CENODOXUS: Frugalis est & coena mihi; Nunquam meis
    Opipara mensis inferuntur: Nec novis   255
    Abundo lautitijs. Meri sum parcior,
    Quam sit necesse; paene nostrum abstemium
    Ut prandium sit fas vocare: Socratem
    Aliquem referre videor.
PHILAUTIA: Apage Socratem,

SELF-LOVE: Whom sanctity itself
   Is honoured by!
CENODOXUS: A light to lighten France?
SELF-LOVE: The sun itself.
CENODOXUS: The conscience of the king?
SELF-LOVE: The realm's salvation!
CENODOXUS: This and more they say.
   I'd stop at nothing to be so esteemed.
SELF-LOVE: To appear like this is sweet; for this no price
   Could be too great.
CENODOXUS: Wakeful and easeless are
   My days and nights, consumed in careful studies.
SELF-LOVE: But time cannot consume what all men's praises
   Render immortal.
CENODOXUS: Yet how easily
   Such honours can be gained. My life's whole purpose
   Is therefore this: by glorious deeds to ensure
   That I and all my glory never perish.
   This die I've cast.
SELF-LOVE: Nor even if you wished it
   Could this fame be concealed; this virtue in you
   Has to be cherished, whether you will or no.
CENODOXUS: Eternal ruler of the world! What thanks
   Can I return you for these crowning virtues
   Which make me the envy of all, while envying none?
SELF-LOVE: A mind like this is worth such worthy fortune.
CENODOXUS: See how the poor and needy come to me,
   Approach me as a father, with prayers, entreaties,
   Offering me praise and love; their poverty
   I succour with my wealth; not even suffering
   Their prayers for alms, my generous right hand
   Seems anxious to anticipate such prayers.
SELF-LOVE: Piety itself would yield the palm to you.
CENODOXUS: I keep a frugal board; no sumptuous dishes
   Burden my table; nor do I make a show
   Of fashionable elegance; sparing of wine
   More than is needful, it might well be said,
   Abstemiousness rules my board; to some
   I seem another Socrates.
SELF-LOVE: What, Socrates!

Qui comparari, si tibi velit, bibo,   260
Mando, gulo, helluo, nepos videbitur.
CENODOXUS: Jam quanta res est, in secunda gloria
Inque omnium acclamationibus, nihil
Turgere fastu; ferre eo moderatius
Superos faventes, quo favent mage: nimias   265
Felicitates sic amare, ut metuere
Videaris; itaque prosperis rebus frui,
Ut & carere noveris? quibus equidem
Rebus operam simul ita navavi omnibus,
Ut singulis dedisse totam crederer.   270
PHILAUTIA: Laus rara, multis vendicata perperam;
Hic vera; veriorque, si major foret.
CENODOXUS: His, tamque honestis coepi ego studijs meam
Ad gloriam grassari. Et haud mirum est, ijs
Homines moveri, meque amari ob talia: 275
DEO haec probari etiam liquet.
PHILAUTIA: Nihil ut supra.
CENODOXUS: Nunc ego labore fessus, in pomoerium
Secedo, scena ut recreem me umbratili.

SCENA IV
DAMA, CENODOXUS, MARISCUS,
LABEO, NASO, Famuli,
DROPAX, SMILAX, Lictores

DAMA: Estne alicubi in propinquo herus? Nusquam hac ijt?
CENODOXUS: Dama.   280
DAMA: Ecquis appellat? Herus ipse est; salva res.
CENODOXUS: Quidnam est necesse?
DAMA: Magna vis mortalium
Primis in aedibus moratur, omnium
Votum est, te adire.
CENODOXUS: Cui rei?
DAMA: Alij ut consulant;
Alij ut rogent; nonnemo qui donarijs
Colat; pari omnes pertinacia in statu   285
Manent: abire se negant posse antea,
Quam te potiti, rebus consulant suis.
CENODOXUS: Etiamne Principes viri aliqui?

Compared with you he's nothing but a sot,
Base, tippling, drunken, spendthrift, guzzling glutton.

CENODOXUS: How great a thing it is, when fortune smiles,
And all acclaim me, not to be puffed up
With pride; to accept of Heaven's gracious favour
More modestly, the more it favours me;
To love such blessings, so that it appears
I shun them; bask in prosperity and yet
Seem not to care for it. So have I striven
In practising these virtues that I seem
To give my all to each and every one.

SELF-LOVE: Rare praise indeed, which many falsely claim;
But this would still be true, if even greater.

CENODOXUS: So, and so honestly, have I endeavoured
To grasp at glory; nor is it any wonder
That men are moved by this and love me for it.
God too must give His blessing.

SELF-LOVE: The supreme goal.

CENODOXUS: Now I am weary with toil and will retreat
To seek refreshment in my garden's shade.

SCENE IV
DAMA, CENODOXUS, MARISCUS,
LABEO, NASO, slaves,
DROPAX, SMILAX, lictors

DAMA: Is master here, or has he been around?

CENODOXUS: Dama!

DAMA: Who's calling? What a relief! It's him.

CENODOXUS: What's the matter?

DAMA: A great crowd of men
Is waiting at the door, all wanting to
Consult you.

CENODOXUS: What about?

DAMA: Some seek advice,
Some help, and quite a few bring gifts to gain
Your grace; all doggedly rooted to the spot,
Declaring that they will not go away
Until they've seen you and been aided by you.

CENODOXUS: Any distinguished men among them?

DAMA: Principes
Sane.

CENODOXUS: Est, quod aio: Auxilia, consilia rogor
  Noctes diesque. Prope togatam operam mihi   290
  Alij, alijs ego praesto. Abi, dic me affore.

DAMA: Eo: sed eorum memorat unus, quid tuo
  Marisco evenerit hodie; quem in prandium
  Tota urbe quaeritando, nusquam inveneram.

CENODOXUS: Laetum aliquid?   295

DAMA: Adeo triste. Nam forte in canem
  Rabie ferocem illatus, ab eo admorsus est.

CENODOXUS: Facilis medela est.

DAMA: Sed malum ille primitus
  Contemsit, ut ne timidus esset. Altera
  Hora deinde, & ipse rabie percitus
  Furere palam occoepit; per urbem currere,   300
  Clamare, despumare, caedere obvios.
  Caveto proinde ab homine, jam minime homine;
  Fera est, feraque immanior.

CENODOXUS: Mihi dolitum est
  Hominis vicem.

DAMA: Eccum, incoram adest; ut diffluit
  Sudore? ut intorquet oculos!   305

MARISCUS: Ego, ego; ego, ego.

DAMA: Audin'?

MARISCUS: Ego puerum hunc.

DAMA: Viden', ut ambas manus
  Projectat?

CENODOXUS: Ego formido; famulos evoca.

MARISCUS: In frustra puerum hunc flagrionem, simul eum
  Invenero, concerpam? ita ille me?

DAMA: Foras
  Naso, Labeo; foras.   310

NASO, LABEO: Quid est? quid facto opus?

CENODOXUS: Modo respicit.

DAMA: Etiam advenit.

CENODOXUS: Resistite.

DAMA: Arcete rabidum hunc, ne propius adeat herum.

MARISCUS: Hoplitodromus Megaloperiphronesterus
  Puer, in Pyrgopolitoxia te perduit.

DAMA: Audin', ut etiam insanit? ut modo tragicas   315
  Voces hiulcat?

DAMA: Leading men
    Indeed.

CENODOXUS: It's as I say. They seek my help
    And counsel night and day, as if I were
    Official Counsellor. Tell them I'm coming.

DAMA: Yes. Oh, and one of them told me what happened
    This morning to Mariscus. All in vain
    I searched the town to bring him here to lunch.

CENODOXUS: Good news?

DAMA: No, rather sad. They say he met
    A dog with rabies and got bitten by it.

CENODOXUS: That's easily cured.

DAMA: He pooh-poohed it at first,
    Not wanting to seem cowardly. An hour passed,
    And then the madness struck him, so that raving
    Quite obviously, and rushing through the town,
    He foamed and shouted, hitting out at people.
    Be wary of this man–well hardly 'man',
    He's a wild animal, only rather wilder.

CENODOXUS: Poor fellow!

DAMA: But here he is. See how the sweat
    Is pouring off him, how he rolls his eyes!

MARISCUS: I, I...

DAMA: Do you hear him?

MARISCUS: That slave I'll ...

DAMA: See how with both his hands
    He flails the air.

CENODOXUS: I'm frightened; call the slaves.

MARISCUS: I'll make mince-meat of that wretch once I can get
    My hands on him. He dares to...

DAMA: Come out here,
    Naso, Labeo, come out.

NASO, LABEO: Why? What's happening?

CENODOXUS: He's looking round.

DAMA: Advancing!

CENODOXUS: Keep him off.

DAMA: Don't let this lunatic come any closer.

MARISCUS: Hoplitodromus Megaloperiphronesterus,
    Boy, may he do for you in Pyrgopolitoxia.

DAMA: You hear his ravings? How he utters bits
    Of mangled tragedy?

MARISCUS: Hunc, sinite jam me, ut neci
        Dem puerum.
LABEO: Omitte.
MARISCUS: Qui adeo me?
DAMA: Vehemens dolor,
        Credo, haud sinit loqui.
MARISCUS: Loquar mox cum tuo
        Malo.
NASO: Recede.
MARISCUS: Tamdiu me infra, supra;
        Retro, ante; & extra, & intus; & procul & prope.   320
DAMA: Nihil cohaeret: ut potens rabies malum est?
MARISCUS: Per septa, compita, fora, vicos, porticus
        Me circumagebas.
DAMA: Nempe morbus imaginem
        Illi meam objecit: putabat me insequi,
        Seseque verberare: facile ignoscere est;   325
        Nam talia evenire ferme usuvenit
        Amentibus.
CENODOXUS: Id est simile vero. Astringite
        Utrinque fortius.
MARISCUS: Sinite; quae noxia est
        Mea? quod piaculum? tuam appello fidem
        Cenodoxe, quid commerui?   330
CENODOXUS: In ipsa insania
        Meminit tamen nomen meum. Quid non facit
        Amor?
DAMA: Ego vix a lacrimis mihi tempero,
        Cum cogito hunc sapientem heri, repente jam
        Ita furere.
MARISCUS: Quis enim furit, nequissime?
        Ego caput effringam tibi, simul ac ero   335
        Liber.
DAMA: Tenete, quaeso, ne liber siet.
CENODOXUS: Includite illum ergastulo, ne cui manus
        Forte afferat.
MARISCUS: Cenodoxe, an etiam tu furis?
DAMA: Ignosce, ita solet morbus. En ut dentibus
        Infrendat?   340
MARISCUS: Obsecro, date loquendi moram.
        Nunquid ego sum furiosus? ut qui ita singula

MARISCUS: Just let me cook
     His goose.
LABEO: Stop that.
MARISCUS: You dare…?
DAMA: His sad affliction
     Chokes back his words.
MARISCUS: I'll soon speak out and you
     Will suffer for it.
NASO: Back!
MARISCUS: Hours up and down,
     Back, forth, in, out, here, there and everywhere.
DAMA: He can't talk sense: it's terrible, this rabies!
MARISCUS: Driving me on through alleys, cross-roads, streets,
     Gateways and squares.
DAMA: His ailment made him think
     He saw me, and he thought that I was chasing
     And flogging him. He's easily forgiven,
     For madmen very often are deluded
     By wild imaginings.
CENODOXUS   Likely enough.
     Hold him more tightly.
MARISCUS: Stop; what have I done
     What crime have I committed, or what punishment
     Deserved, Cenodoxus?
CENODOXUS: Even in such madness
     My name is memorable. What can love not do?
DAMA: I can hardly hold back tears, when I reflect
     That this man, so wise yesterday, is now
     Suddenly raving mad.
MARISCUS: Who's mad, you wretch?
     I'll break your head in, just as soon as I
     Get free.
DAMA: Make sure he's not free, pray.
CENODOXUS: Best put him behind bars, before he goes
     Attacking someone.
MARISCUS: You mad too, Cenodoxus?
DAMA: Forgive him, it's because he's sick. Hear how
     He grinds his teeth.
MARISCUS: Please give me leave to speak.
     You say I'm mad? When I can quote each word

Amussitate noverim, quae dixeras
Mihi Dama?
DAMA: Quaenam illa? cedo.
MARISCUS: Bromius ut hodie
Conciderit exanimis?
LABEO: Stetit, si unquam antea.
DAMA: Viden', ut memoriam etiam malum expugnaverit?   345
Quid porro?
MARISCUS: Domus ut esse subito pestilens
Inceperit?
CENODOXUS: Nihil.
MARISCUS: Ut domo emigraveris?
CENODOXUS: Nihil.
MARISCUS: Ut suburbanum petiveris?
CENODOXUS: Nihil.
MARISCUS: Nihil, nihil, nihil, nihil; ego utique scio!
CENODOXUS: Lepida boni hominis somnia: Neque enim accidit   350
Quicquam omnium horum.
NASO: Luculenta insania est.
MARISCUS: Vestra, autumno: nam mea quidem nulla, liquido, est.
DAMA: Arctate brachia. Quam laborat?
CENODOXUS: Ducite
Ut imperavi. Ego abeo visum, quid rogent,
Qui me intus opperiuntur. Hac Dama sequere.   355
MARISCUS: Cives, fidem vestram.
NASO: Labeo, nisi viribus
Totis vir es, nihil agimus.
LABEO: Connitere
Naso; mihi nunquam ille excidet, licet altero
Tanto impotentius furat.
MARISCUS: Cives, fidem
Vestram; opitulamini innocenti.   360
NASO: Rectius,
Insanienti.
DROPAX: Quid sibi haec contentio?
MARISCUS: Insanus habeor, qui neque modo sum, neque
Olim fui unquam. Quaeso, vos, anne videor
Insanus esse?
SMILAX: Propemodum.
LABEO: A rabido cane
Miser modo est invasus.   365

> And syllable that Dama said to me?

DAMA: All right, quote on!

MARISCUS: How Bromius this morning
>   Fell down and died?

LABEO: He's well if ever he was.

DAMA: See how the malady attacks his memory.
>   What else?

MARISCUS: How suddenly the house was struck
>   By plague?

CENODOXUS: No, no.

MARISCUS: And so you left the house?

CENODOXUS: No.

MARISCUS: For your place outside the town?

CENODOXUS: No, no.

MARISCUS: No, no, no, no!–but I know it must be so!

CENODOXUS: The good man's dreaming. None of this is true.

NASO: It's obvious he's gone right off his head.

MARISCUS: You mean you have. It's clear that I'm quite sane.

DAMA: Hold his arms tight. Look at him struggling.

CENODOXUS: Take him.
>   Where I have told you. I'll investigate
>   The wishes of my waiting clients. Come, Dama.

MARISCUS: Citizens, help!

NASO: You must use all your strength,
>   Labeo, or we're done for.

LABEO: Use all yours,
>   Naso, as well. He'll not escape us both
>   Even if he's twice as mad.

MARISCUS: Citizens, help me,
>   Help a guiltless man.

NASO: A mindless one,
>   You mean.

DROPAX: What's all this noise about?

MARISCUS: They think
>   I'm mad, but I am not, nor ever have been.
>   I ask you, does it look as if I'm mad?

SMILAX: It does a bit.

LABEO: He's just been set upon,
>   Poor man, by a mad dog.

MARISCUS: Ego?
LABEO: Tu tu.
MARISCUS: Canem
Ego triduo nusquam attigi ullum.
DROPAX: Dummodo
Te, stulte, canis attigerit.
SMILAX: Apparet satis,
Hunc furere.
MARISCUS: Non furo: sinite.
NASO: Dropax, cave
Ne admordeat; sunt virulentae talium
Commorsiones.   370
DROPAX: Illi ego, ubi tentaverit,
Dolabo dentes ferreo hoc manubrio.
SMILAX: Agite ergo; caveam in publicam deducitor,
Ubi caeteri attinentur hoc genus homines.
MARISCUS: Non eo.
DROPAX: Feremus; habe bonum animum.
MARISCUS: Non eo.

SCENA V
CENODOXOPHYLAX, CONSCIENTIA

CENODOXOPHYLAX: In tempore adsum, alumno ut afferam meo   375
Adversus acies inferas praesentem opem.
Illum ambiunt occulta monstra, & impetunt
Mille artibus, praeceps ut eat. O improbos
Orci labores! vigilat hostis pervigil
In perniciem hominis; & homo tamen sui   380
Securus altum stertit! Ah quoties male
Periret ille, nostra nisi defenderet
Tutela? lapsu, fraude, ferro, toxico
Periclitatur in dies; nescit tamen
Cujus ope vincat: sed sciet quondam, sciet.   385
Ego Cenodoxum vindicatum eo jam; ades
Huc Conscientia; subi in has aedes; subi.
CONSCIENTIA: Quid ibi imperas praestare?
CENODOXOPHYLAX: Cenodoxon meum
Urgeto stimulis; inquietum reddito,
Timere discat, quando amare non cupit.   390

MARISCUS: What, me?

LABEO: Yes, you.

MARISCUS: I haven't touched a dog for three whole days.

DROPAX: The dog touched you, you fool.

SMILAX: It's clear enough,
     The man is mad.

MARISCUS: I'm sane. Stop this.

NASO: Dropax,
     Take care he doesn't bite you. Madmen's bites
     Are dangerous.

DROPAX: Just let him try that on.
     I'll bash his teeth in with this metal bar.

SMILAX: Let's go then. Take him to the loony bin,
     Where they keep other loonies.

MARISCUS: I won't go.

DROPAX: Well then, we'll carry you. Cheer up.

MARISCUS: No, no.

SCENE V
CENODOXOPHYLAX, CONSCIENCE

CENODOXOPHYLAX: I come betimes to bring help to my ward,
     Myself in person, against the hosts of hell.
     Forces occult encompass him, employing
     A thousand wiles to bring about his fall.
     Oh impious toils of Orcus! Ever wakeful
     Man's foe awaits man's fall, while careless man
     Heedlessly snores away. Alas, how often
     Would he have perished, had our watchful care
     Not guarded him? Each day he is in peril
     From treachery, poison and the sword, not knowing
     By whose aid he survives. He'll know one day.
     I'm here now to look after Cenodoxus.
     Be with me, Conscience; come into this house.

CONSCIENCE: What do you bid me do there?

CENODOXOPHYLAX: With your pangs
     Beset my Cenodoxus, make him anxious,
     Let him learn fear, since he denies us love.

CONSCIENTIA: Id sponte soleo mea: proin' ego naviter
    Curabo.
CENODOXOPHYLAX: Torque, adhaere, inhaere: nec prius
    Desiste, quam ille absistat. Habeat vulturem
    Hunc Tityus. Hos consuevimus nos Caelites
    Hominum animis subinde punctus indere.   395
    Sed, pro dolor! contemnere illos jam sciunt;
    Nos fungimur nostrum tamen munus. Quid hoc,
    Quod contuor? Ubique laquei, circum has vias;
    Quos, nisi oculos mille habeat, ah nemo fugiet.
    Scio, scio; Cenodoxum petunt, ut se induat.   400
    O si videret! sed nihil ago; homo non videt,
    Nos Caelites videmus. Ego tamen ut juvem
    In parte, laqueos inter istos semina
    Interseram aliqua, quae videat & reperiat;
    Casuque factum existimet, quod feci ego.   405
    Ah crescite in messem, atque maturescite.

SCENA VI
PANURGUS, HYPOCRISIS, PHILAUTIA

PANURGUS: Hui quanta pandit ora, quantis increpat
    Rictibus Avernus? Glutit, haurit, devorat;
    Nec ulla satias implet illam belluae
    Voraginem. Sitit bibendo, & esurit   410
    Vorando. Quicquid ingero, diram famem
    Accendit. Omnes undique socij mei
    Quaerunt, ferunt, trahuntque rapiuntque omnia;
    Tantusque continenter ingruit hominum
    Ruentium imber, ut obstupescam quempiam   415
    Terris superstitem inveniri. Sicubi
    Emergo rursus has in auras, illico
    Superesse tantum segetis admiror Stygi,
    Ac si fuisset nulla messis hactenus.
    Poene nihil opus est viribus meis: sua   420
    Plerique sponte pessum eunt. Hinc pauculi
    Caeco resistunt Marte; quos Philautia
    Hypocrisisque facile transversos agunt.
    Sed fallor, an recentia superi alitis
    Adverto vestigia? profecto jam adfuit   425

CONSCIENCE: I've done this on my own initiative,
    And gladly shall again.
CENODOXOPHYLAX: Invade and torment
    His soul unceasingly, until he cease
    To sin. Let Tityus have this vulture. Thus
    With stings we angels goad the minds of men
    Unceasingly. Alas, they soon despise them.
    We will discharge our duty none the less.
    What do I see? Snares all around the house?
    Without a thousand eyes none could escape them!
    I see it all. They're traps for Cenodoxus.
    I can do nothing when a mortal's blind;
    Could he but see as we do! Yet I'll help him.
    Among these snares I'll sow some seeds, which he
    May see and find, supposing that mere chance,
    Which I have done on purpose. May they then
    Ripen and grow apace and bear rich fruit.

SCENE VI
PANURGUS, HYPOCRISY, SELF-LOVE

PANURGUS: How cavernous the maw, how vast the gulf
    Of gaping-jawed Avernus, whose great gorge
    Devours continually without satiety!
    Gulping it thirsts, and though devouring, starves.
    Whatever we feed into it inflames
    Its fearful hunger. Everywhere my comrades
    Seek, hunt, seize, snatch and harry all mankind;
    So vast the surge of human souls that rains
    Continuously down on us, I marvel
    That there are any left here on the earth.
    Wherever I re-emerge in upper air
    I wonder that so great a Stygian crop
    Still stands uncut as if there'd been no harvest.
    My help is hardly needed; most of them
    Go freely to perdition. Just a few
    Blindly put up a fight, and they are easily
    Thwarted by Self-Love and Hypocrisy.
    But am I wrong or do I recognise
    Some recent signs of heavenly visitation?

Hostis meus; domum hanc nove communijt:
Neque enim aditus ita huc liber est, ut anteidhac
Fuit. Repellor viribus tacitis ego,
Heu me! male olim hoc metui, ut ille ne meam
Praedam mihi ereptum iret. Ecce, & chartulas   430
Hic conspicor! bono illius forte positas;
Ita est, ita est: phuj, phuj. Neque licet tollere.
Jam sentio quid agatur intus! Hypocrisis,
Philautia, huc adeste; confestim; mora
Quae demoratur? Hypocrisis, Philautia   435
Adeste, adeste, surda utraque. Quis detinet?
Quae vis manusve injecta? Praesto huc utraque.
Neque dum etiam? Parere jam demum negant,
Parere semper suetae; & alias obviae
Ubique, nunc sunt nuspiam? Juro piceos   440
Lacus, & antra nocte jugi horrentia!
Philautia, Hypocrisis venite.
HYPOCRISIS: Quae, malum
    Venire nos jubet, vetatque necessitas?
PHILAUTIA: Cenodoxus hinc trahit; retrahit alia huc manus.
PANURGUS: Ego evocavi utramque. Nam summi ducis   445
    Imperia meque vosque pariter attinent.
    Quid distulistis?
HYPOCRISIS: Occupabamur adeo
PANURGUS: Id est, quod aveo scire.
HYPOCRISIS: Cenodoxo fuit
    Danda opera.
PANURGUS: Recte istuc quidem: sed quid spei est?
PHILAUTIA: Nutare coepit, neque ita nobis libere   450
    Obtemperare.
PANURGUS: Nempe quia vos languidae
    Cessastis?
HYPOCRISIS: Imo quia tu ad has fores iners
    Excubitor adstitisti, & hostem huc ingredi
    Sivisti.
PANURGUS: An alitem inquis illum caelitum;
HYPOCRISIS: Hunc, inquio; at non solum.   455
PANURGUS: Etiam alium? cedo
    Quem?
HYPOCRISIS: Conscientiam.
PANURGUS: Male, male, male, male.
    Indene movetur?

My enemy has fortified this house.
There's no free access to it, as there once was.
Hidden, repelling forces hold me back.
I feared my prey might suddenly be snatched
Away from me. And here are texts, I see,
Strewn round for him to find and profit from.
That's it! Nor can I wipe them out or move them.
Now I can see what's going on inside!
Hasten Self-Love, Hypocrisy! Come here!
Why this delay? Come, both of you, at once!
Come here! They must be deaf. What's keeping them?
What force delays them? Come here, both of you!
No sign of them? Do they refuse to be here?
They who were always everywhere? Now nowhere?
Such omnipresent entities quite absent?
By lakes of pitch and caves of endless night,
I summon Self-Love and Hypocrisy!

HYPOCRISY: What? Evil bids us come when fate forbids?

SELF-LOVE: We're drawn to, and withdrawn from, Cenodoxus.

PANURGUS: I called you both. Our sovereign leader's orders
Concern both you and me, and equally.
Why the delay?

HYPOCRISY: We both had work to do.

PANURGUS: What kind of work, I ask?

HYPOCRISY: We had to work
On Cenodoxus.

PANURGUS: Rightly. What hope is there?

SELF-LOVE: Faltering a little, he's less willing now
To serve us.

PANURGUS: That's no doubt because you've been
Remiss and slack!

HYPOCRISY: You mean because you watched
So feebly, that the enemy came in
Straight through the door.

PANURGUS: That angel, do you mean?

HYPOCRISY: Yes, and not only that one.

PANURGUS: What? Who else then?

HYPOCRISY: Who else? Why, Conscience.

PANURGUS: Hell! Hell! Hell! Hell!
Hell!
Is he affected?

PHILAUTIA: Nutat ille, & territus
Subinde sistit, & subinde reijcit
Consilia nostra.
PANURGUS: Redite propere: nam in mora
Periculum est. Urgete denuo; omnibus   460
Technis studete, ut Conscientiam domo
Eliminetis: actum agitis, hanc donicum
Vicistis: Ite. Ego interim nihil meo
Referam Imperatori, quoad redeat mihi
Cenodoxus, & ductu meo superbiat.   465
Perij ego, nisi perisse ego illum videro.

SELF-LOVE: Wavering, terrified;
          Now standing firm, now suddenly rejecting
          Our guiding counsels.
PANURGUS: Back to him, quick! Delay
          Is dangerous. Urge him again, use all
          The subtleties your zeal contrives, to rid
          The house of Conscience; otherwise, we're done.
          Now go. I'll not report to our commander
          Until I have my Cenodoxus back
          Playing his game of pride to match my rules.
          I'm damned if I'll see him escape damnation!

ACTUS II

GUARINUS: Miror, Philarete, numinis patientiam;
Matura scelera vindicat tarda manu,
Parcitque, cum parcendo proficiat nihil.
Jam fulminatos orbis omnes angulos   470
Oportuit; moveret ira, quos solet
Clementia efferare.
PHILARETUS: Quid enim displicet
Guarine?
GUARINUS: Philarete, quid enim non displicet?
Non ego placere, non alia mihi queunt.
PHILARETUS: Quae causa?   475
GUARINUS: Tempora, nosq; pejores malis
Temporibus. Exclamare cogor: Viximus,
Unaque vixit probior aetas. Moribus
Vitiatus orbis atque labefactatus est.
Ad summa scelerum venimus. Cui jam fides,
Cui candor est animo? Quis ad modestiam 480
Proclivior? fastum odimus; sed in alijs
Nostrum, fovemus! O scelesta saecula!
Quae vos cicuta purget!
PHILARETUS: Hic convitium
Ne facito. Nobilis etiamnum heroicam
Orchestra virtutem videt: Neque penitus 485
Jugulata verso pollice est.
GUARINUS: Utinam quidem
Philarete, vivat: fallere libenter velim.
Sed vereor, & veretur orbis: viribus

Act Two

SCENE I
GUARINUS, PHILARETUS

GUARINUS: Philaretus, I marvel at God's patience:
      Ripe crimes are punished with so slow a hand,
      And malefactors spared to sin again.
      The whole world should be struck with thunderbolts,
      God's anger shaking those whose vicious ways
      His clemency encourages.
PHILARETUS: What is it?
      What makes you so displeased?
GUARINUS: Ah, what does not?
      Not I myself nor anything can please me.
PHILARETUS: But why?
GUARINUS: The times are evil, so are we,
      And worsening with the times. We've finished living,
      And so has probity. This must be said:
      The world is vitiated, vile and ruinous.
      Our crimes have reached their peak. Where now is found
      Integrity and trust? Who now inclines
      To modesty? We hate pride, but in others;
      Our own, we cherish! Wicked, impious age!
      What hemlock shall purge you?
PHILARETUS: Spare your reproofs:
      A noble audience can still descry
      Heroic virtue, nor must we pronounce
      Death sentence on ourselves.
GUARINUS: Oh, but Philaretus,
      If only there were any signs of life
      I'd gladly own myself to be mistaken;
      But my fear, and the world's, is that no force

Restitui in integrum potest nullis. Pedes
Extendit alto collocata lectulo   490
Probitas: quid esse jam super sperabimus?
PHILARETUS: Pios viros, & sanctitate principes.
GUARINUS: Verum nec ita multos.
PHILARETUS: Nec ita paucos tamen.
Cenodoxon, inquam: cujus uno nomine
Jam te refelli.   495
GUARINUS: Fateor; ille quidem parem
Et sanctitatem, & eruditionem habet:
Sed unus. Utinam potius unum diceres
Esse improbum e multis bonis; quam unum bonum
Ex improbis multis.
PHILARETUS: Ubi Cenodoxus est
Vel unus, ibi multos bonos esse autuma.   500
Exemplo enim trahit suo, imo facit bonos.
Placet experiri?
GUARINUS: Quomodo?
PHILARETUS: Ad Philedemonem
Hac sequere: quicum Bruno & Hugo & caeteri
Pro more, & eruditionis gratia
Post paululum intervisere illum cogitant.   505
Si litteras amas, adire & tu potes.
GUARINUS: Sequar ergo, ubi esse bonus apud bonos sciam.

SCENA II
GUARINUS, PHILARETUS, MARISCUS

GUARINUS: Sed ecquis inde ad nos?
PHILARETUS: Mariscus aedibus
Illis beatis exit. O te prosperum
Marisce!   510
MARISCUS: Quid ita?
PHILARETUS: Qui huic viro unus omnium
Es intimus.
MARISCUS: Cui? quaeso.
PHILARETUS: Cenodoxo. An vacat
Jam conveniri?
MARISCUS: Mox vacabit: sunt enim
Modo in abitu, qui gravibus in negotijs
Illum hactenus tenuere.

Can bring it back to life, and Probity
Aloof upon its couch, lies mute and dormant.
What hope's left?

PHILARETUS: Men of holy piety.

GUARINUS: There are not so many of those.

PHILARETUS: Nor yet so few.
Let me name Cenodoxus; he alone
Serves to refute you.

GUARINUS: True. He's blessed with learning
And sanctity; but he is only one!
Better one bad man among many good,
Than only one good among many bad.

PHILARETUS: Where Cenodoxus is, though he's but one,
Count on it, many good men will be found.
For his example draws good men – and makes them!
Shall we put it to the test?

GUARINUS: How?

PHILARETUS: Come with me
To Philedemones. He, Bruno, Hugo,
And others are about to visit him,
To learn from him, as they so often do.
If you love learning, come with us.

GUARINUS: I will,
Knowing, a good man, I'll be with good men there.

SCENE II
GUARINUS, PHILARETUS, MARISCUS

GUARINUS: But who's this coming?

PHILARETUS: It's Mariscus, leaving
That blessed house. How fortunate you are,
Mariscus!

MARISCUS: Why?

PHILARETUS: Because you are so close
To this man.

MARISCUS: Who?

PHILARETUS: Cenodoxus. Is he free
To welcome guests?

MARISCUS: He'll soon be free. The people
Who've kept him, up till now, with serious business
Are just about to leave.

GUARINUS: At ego te gratulor
    Marisce sospitem esse.   515
MARISCUS: Me? nunquam male
    Mihi fuit.
GUARINUS: Atqui non furit quisquam sine
    Dolore.
MARISCUS: Quis me enim furere dixit?
GUARINUS: Parum
    Duntaxat. Etquod remedium morbi fuit?
MARISCUS: Cujus?
GUARINUS: Furoris.
MARISCUS: Nullo opus erat.
GUARINUS: Scilicet
    Sponte redijsti ad mentem?   520
MARISCUS: At ego nunquam excidi.
GUARINUS: Scio erubescis. Quanquam id humanum est, pati
    Perinde nos, & erubescere talia.
    Sed frustra es. Omnes obvij factum sciunt.
MARISCUS: Falsum sciunt.
GUARINUS: Narrant tamen vulgo & putant.
MARISCUS: Quo auctore?   525
GUARINUS: Dama.
MARISCUS: Nequius puero est nihil.
PHILARETUS: Damane?
MARISCUS: Dama. Nam ille me urbi fabulam hanc
    Fecit, libidine ductus & licentia
    Vernili. At ultus sum, simul cum compedes
    Hodie exui. Graviter enim admodum tulit
    Cenodoxus, ita sibi & mihi mastigiam   530
    Os sublinere voluisse. Quare invasimus
    Uterque puerum, palma, fuste, taurea,
    Quod cuique telum. Vix putem pro Troja
    Plura esse tela aut capta quondam, aut perdita,
    Quam perdiderimus uno in illo. Caeterum   535
    Vos sapere me putate.
PHILARETUS: Si tu id publicis
    Tabulis doces, credemus. Interea loci
    Perendinamus causam.
MARISCUS: Ita placet. Nunc voco
    Philedemonem ad Cenodoxon.
PHILARETUS: Eodem intendimus.

GUARINUS: I'm pleased to see
    You're well again.
MARISCUS: What me? I've not been ill.
GUARINUS: A man who's mad can hardly be quite well!
MARISCUS: Who said that I've been mad?
GUARINUS: Just slightly mad.
    What remedy did you use?
MARISCUS: What for?
GUARINUS: Your madness.
MARISCUS: I didn't need one.
GUARINUS: What, you found your wits, then,
    Quite spontaneously?
MARISCUS: I never lost them.
GUARINUS: You're obviously embarrassed. Yet it's human
    To be ashamed of suffering such things.
    But it's no good. The whole town knows the facts.
MARISCUS: They're wrong.
GUARINUS: They're common knowledge.
MARISCUS: Oh, who told
    you?
GUARINUS: Dama.
MARISCUS: That slave's a good-for-nothing rogue.
PHILARETUS: Dama?
MARISCUS: Yes, Dama. He's the one who spread
    This tale about me, wicked wily liar
    That he is. But once they let me loose today
    I paid him back. For not at all amused
    Was Cenodoxus, that he'd fooled us both.
    And so we both set on the boy with sticks,
    Whips, cudgels, anything that we could find
    To thrash him with. I hardly think more weapons
    Were seized or lost at Troy, than we used up
    On him alone. So now you know I'm sane.
PHILARETUS: Well, put it on the public notice-board
    And we'll believe you. In the meantime let's
    Await events.
MARISCUS: Yes. I'll fetch Philedemones
    To Cenodoxus.
PHILARETUS: We are going too.

SCENA III
CENODOXUS, PHILAUTIA, DAMA

CENODOXUS: Abiere? Superi! omnia mihi negotia   540
   Peragenda soli.
PHILAUTIA: Solus illud scilicet
   Debes, quod & solus potes.
CENODOXUS: Nemo satius
   Fecisset, equidem opinor. Ego Rempublicam,
   Ego Regna, privatasque caussas tantulo
   Spatio expedivi. Usque adeo, nil decidere,   545
   Suadere, persuadere, conficere, mihi est
   Difficile.
PHILAUTIA: Solum difficile tibi est, alijs
   Deesse.
CENODOXUS: Ades dum Dama.
DAMA: Quid facto est opus?
CENODOXUS: Abiere?
DAMA: Jam nunc.
CENODOXUS: Colloquentes videram
   Inter abeundum: quid ferebant?   550
DAMA: Laudibus
   Te, here, extulere.
PHILAUTIA: Merita nullis laudibus
   Tua pariabunt.
CENODOXUS: Perge porro; quid dein?
DAMA: Prudentiam tibi singularem a Numine
   Esse inditam, dixere, qua plerisque alijs
   Excelleres.   555
PHILAUTIA: Plerisque tantum? imo omnibus.
DAMA: Tum comitatem, & inclyti modestiam
   Ingenij praedicabant: esseque dubium
   Prudentiorne, doctiorne an comior
   Fores?
PHILAUTIA: Dubia cum palma multis redditur
   Virtutibus, meruere palmam singulae.   560
CENODOXUS: Nihil aliud dixere?
DAMA: Multas insuper
   Laudes recensuere, tibique proprias.
CENODOXUS: Narra.
DAMA: Exciderunt.

SCENE III
CENODOXUS, SELF-LOVE, DAMA

CENODOXUS: All gone? Good heavens, every single detail
    Must be attended to by me alone.
SELF-LOVE: By you alone, for only you can do it.
CENODOXUS: None better, certainly. Affairs of state,
    Public and private matters I and I
    Alone have dealt with expeditiously.
    Simple for me to counsel, plan, decide,
    Conclude affairs.
SELF-LOVE: Your only difficulty
    Is *not* to help others.
CENODOXUS: Dama!
DAMA: Yes, what is it?
CENODOXUS: Have they all gone?
DAMA: Yes, now.
CENODOXUS: I saw them talking
    As they went off. What did they say?
DAMA: They praised you
    To the skies.
SELF-LOVE: No praises can approximate
    Your merits.
CENODOXUS: Well, go on. What then?
DAMA: They said
    What singular prudence have the heavenly powers
    Endowed you with, so that you far excel
    Most others.
SELF-LOVE: Only most? Why surely all!
DAMA: Your courtesy they praised, your modest bearing
    Of your great fame, uncertain whether prudence,
    Culture or courtesy were your crowning quality.
SELF-LOVE: Such crowning qualities as these contending
    Must merit each an individual crown.
CENODOXUS: Did they say nothing else?
DAMA: A great deal more:
    They sang your many praises, one by one.
CENODOXUS: Such as?
DAMA: They've slipped my mind.

CENODOXUS: Itane; verbero? oportuit
   Haec excidere?
DAMA: Quis omnium tandem queat
   Meminisse?   565
CENODOXUS: Faxo, nunquam ut hodie verberum
   Oblitteres memoriam. Adeone multae erant?
DAMA: Opinor.
CENODOXUS: En scelus scelestum; Nisi hodie
   Mihi singula edis adamussim, tum nihil edes.
PHILAUTIA: Jure facis: & graviorem isthuic piaculo
   Multam irrogasses, nisi nimis facilis fores.   570
DAMA: Lex dura. Caenitare, Dama, si cupis
   Loquaris opus est. Quid loquar? quando nihil est
   Quod quis loquatur. Nil subit: nihil scio.
   Eho stupor, nihilne quod dicas, scias?
   Si nil adest quod dicam, erit quod mentiar: 575
   Vetus haec mihi est annona. Jam scio; suas
   Audire laudes gestit herus, & promtius
   Credere. Placet. Mentibor, & coenabo. Emam
   Mendacijs, quod alij emunt pecunijs.
CENODOXUS: Quid muginaris interim, scelus!   580
DAMA: Dolet
   Ita excidisse, quod decebat mordicus
   Tenere.
CENODOXUS: Non tibi impune erit.
DAMA: At jam jam, here,
   Subit.
CENODOXUS: Quid ergo?
DAMA: Me beatum serio
   Dixere, qui te abuterer hero.
CENODOXUS: Nec tuam
   Noscis, sceleste, beatitudinem.   585
PHILAUTIA: Tuam
   Tu nosce; fruere.
DAMA: Postibus dein oscula
   Fixere crebra; & inquilinum hunc sospitem
   Et perpetem optabant. Quia gravius tibi
   Si forsitan quid eveniret, nuspiam
   Fore alterum, ad quem se reciperet Civitas.   590
PHILAUTIA: Sapiunt.
CENODOXUS: Profecto, non facile geminum mihi

CENODOXUS: You idiot,
  How dare you let them!
DAMA: Who could possibly
  Remember all of them?
CENODOXUS: I'll see you're thrashed
  So you'll remember it! Were there so many?
DAMA: I think so.
CENODOXUS: Wretch! Recount each one in detail
  Or count yourself out of your food today.
SELF-LOVE: Quite right. A crime like this would have deserved
  Worse punishment, were you not all too lenient.
DAMA: A hard rule, that. If Dama wants to dine,
  He'll have to talk. But what about? When nobody
  Says anything, I can't think what to say.
  Idiot! Can't you think up anything?
  There's nothing true, so I'll just have to lie.
  I've often earned my keep like this. I know:
  My master wants to hear his praises sung.
  He'll lap them up. All right, I'll lie and dine.
  I'll buy with lies what others buy with cash.
CENODOXUS: What are you waiting for, you wretch?
DAMA: I'm sorry,
  It's on the tip of my tongue, but I can't get it out.
CENODOXUS: I'll see you soon regret that.
DAMA: Oh, but now
  It's all come back.
CENODOXUS: Well then?
DAMA: They said how blessed
  I am in having you as master.
CENODOXUS: You
  Can't comprehend how blessed you are!
SELF-LOVE: But you
  Know your own blessedness. Enjoy it.
DAMA: They kissed
  The door repeatedly and wished for you
  A long and happy life, hoping no ill
  Should chance befall you, for no other man
  Was there to whom the state might call for help.
SELF-LOVE: That's wisely said.
CENODOXUS: The state will hardly find

Repererit illa: sed malum tunc sentiet
Suum, mederi nemo cum poterit malo.
PHILAUTIA: Quanti aestimere, cogita.
CENODOXUS: Haec summa?
DAMA: Est, here.
CENODOXUS: Nihil addidere?   595
DAMA: Nihil.
CENODOXUS: Nihil?
PHILAUTIA: Dubio procul
Oblitteravit multa.
DAMA: Plura dixeram,
Quam dixerant.
CENODOXUS: Loquere, scelus.
DAMA: Juro Jovem
Lapidem, nihil superadditum esse quidpiam.
CENODOXUS: Quam pulcra, honesta, sancta res, virtutibus
Ad gloriam eniti? Secus qui abdomini,   600
Gulaeque, aqualiculoque sacrificant suo.
Fato quibuscum nomen interit pari.
Quas vero chartas calco?
PHILAUTIA: Nullius operae.
Omitte.
CENODOXUS: Puer attolle.
PHILAUTIA: Nil, nil dignum habent.
CENODOXUS: Quid profuit nobis superbia?   *Sap.* 5.   605
PHILAUTIA: Abjice.
CENODOXUS: Superbia tua in aures ascendit meas.   *Isa.* 37.
PHILAUTIA: Excute. Nihil juvat has morari inanias.
CENODOXUS: Abominatio Domini omnis arrogans.   *Prov.* 16.
PHILAUTIA: Nihil haec tua intersunt.
CENODOXUS: Tamen aliquid sibi
Volunt: nec est nihilum, quod ita consentiunt.   610
Collige iterum, puer; atque sequere.
DAMA: Colligo.
I nunc, negato obsonium: nunquam meas
Negabo strophas ego, sutelasque tibi.
Tu laude sis, cibarijs ego mavelim
Satur esse. Herum hunc identidem ducto dolis,   615
Quia velle video: & vera laus ubi deficit,
Est assuenda ficta: utraque vanum capit.

        Another like me, and will feel this when
        It tries in vain to remedy my loss.
SELF-LOVE: Know then how high they rate you.
CENODOXUS: Is that all?
DAMA: That's all.
CENODOXUS: No more?
DAMA: No.
CENODOXUS: Nothing else?
SELF-LOVE: No doubt
        He's forgotten a great deal.
DAMA: I said much more
        Than they did.
CENODOXUS: Speak up, boy.
DAMA: So help me, God,
        I've told you every single word there was.
CENODOXUS: How noble, sweet and pious to strive for glory
        Through virtuous practices. How vile are those
        Whose belly, paunch and gullet are their gods.
        Their name dies with them. But what texts are these
        I'm stumbling over?
SELF-LOVE: Take no notice of them.
CENODOXUS: Boy, pick them up.
SELF-LOVE: They're not worth your attention.
CENODOXUS: 'What profits us our pride?'   *Wis.* 5
SELF-LOVE: Throw it away.
CENODOXUS: 'Thy pride has reached my ears.'   *Isa.* 37
SELF-LOVE: Get rid of it.
        It's no good wasting time on trash like that.
CENODOXUS: 'The arrogant are the Lord's abomination.'   *Prov.* 16
SELF-LOVE: These don't concern you.
CENODOXUS: They must have some purpose,
        Nor is it nothing that they all agree.
        Pick them up, boy, and follow me.
DAMA: I will.
        Go on then, stop my food; I'll never stop
        Using my wily tricks on you. You eat
        Your fill of praise, I much prefer to eat
        Real food. I'll feed him up with these delusions
        Since that is what he wants. True praise there's none,
        It has to be made up; it's all delusion.

SCENA IV
CENODOXOPHYLAX, CONSCIENTIA

CENODOXOPHYLAX: Redeo, mei vicem anxius alumni; an velit
    Parere tandem. At lectitavit jam meum
    Schediasma. Placet. O repetat utinam, & sedulus   620
    Perpendat usque, ut arrogantes spiritus
    Demittat olim: Conscientia stimulos
    Fortassis addet, ac reducet in viam.
    O gaudium! Sed ecce, Conscientiam:
    Profecimusne aliquid in Cenodoxo? an manus   625
    Necdum ille dedit?
CONSCIENTIA: Obduruit, & obsurduit,
    Et obstinavit.
CENODOXOPHYLAX: Et recedis?
CONSCIENTIA: Ipsemet
    Recessit; aures mihi negavit; aedibus
    Ejecit. Aliud quid agerem?
CENODOXOPHYLAX: Intro rursum abi;
    Nolens volensque te audiat: clama, obstrepe,   630
    Obtunde; ut efficias nihil, mihi obedies.
CONSCIENTIA: Ingrata & invisa redeo.
CENODOXOPHYLAX: At redi tamen.
    Ego alteram rationem inibo, qua juvem.
    Ah quid hominis causa laboramus! velut
    Si nostra res agatur, omnia facimus,   635
    Ille nihil, & minus nihilo. Erit, heu, erit
    Cum nos rogabit ipse; sed sero nimis.

SCENA V
NAVEGUS, DROPAX, SMILAX

NAVEGUS: Solum salumque obduruit: clementiam
    Expertus utriusque, judico parem
    Esse inclementiam. Mare huc me ejecerat,   640
    Hinc terra me ejicere laborat. Plurimum
    Illic bibendo; hic nihil edendo internecor.
DROPAX: Cuiatis es, homo? quis te in urbem hanc ingredi
    Permisit.
NAVEGUS: Imo etiam coegit.

SCENE IV
CENODOXOPHYLAX, CONSCIENCE

CENODOXOPHYLAX: I come again, concerned about my ward.
      Will he obey at last? He's read my texts.
      That's good. Let him reflect and ponder on them
      With constant zeal, so that the spirit of pride
      Can be cast out by him. Perhaps the stings
      Of Conscience may assist his reformation.
      Oh joyous thought! But here is Conscience now.
      Have we had some success with Cenodoxus?
      Has he yet yielded?
CONSCIENCE: No. Grown hard and stubborn
      His ears are deaf.
CENODOXOPHYLAX: Yet you withdraw?
CONSCIENCE: It's he
      Who has withdrawn from me, turned a deaf ear,
      And turned me out. What else was I to do?
CENODOXOPHYLAX: Go back and *make* him hear you. Shout and cry,
      Bombard his ears. Obey me, though in vain.
CONSCIENCE: I go, unthanked, unwished for.
CENODOXOPHYLAX: But still go.
      I'll help by starting on another plan.
      How hard we labour for the sake of Man!
      We do it all, as if in our own cause,
      While he does nothing, less than nothing. One day
      He'll ask for us himself; but far too late.

SCENE V
NAVEGUS, DROPAX, SMILAX

NAVEGUS: Both sea and shore are hard and cruel; I've tried
      Their mercy, and declare that both alike
      Are merciless. The sea has spewed me out,
      The land tries hard to spew me back. I die,
      By gulping too much there or starving here.
DROPAX: Who are you? Who permitted you to come
      Into this town?
NAVEGUS: Who forced me!

SMILAX: Quis?
NAVEGUS: Fames.
SMILAX: Nihil fames juris habet hoc loci, ut imperet.   645
NAVEGUS: Utinam hic nihil habeat; recedere mox velim.
SMILAX: Nihil habet, inquam, imperia proin tuto potes
    Negligere.
NAVEGUS: Quin summum magistratum hic mihi
    Sese esse dixit.
DROPAX: Male profecto dixit; haud
    Oportuit fidem habere.   650
NAVEGUS: Nimis illa eloquens
    Est visa; persuasit mihi.
DROPAX: Regem hoc loci
    Summum magistratum esse scimus.
NAVEGUS: Recte enim;
    Sed & est fames Regina.
SMILAX: Tollam hinc in malam
    Furcam, tuam hanc Reginam.
NAVEGUS: Amabo. Pessime
    Etenim illa me cruciat. Nam ego illam pro mala   655
    Furca, in malum ventrem egi; abigere inde nequeo.
SMILAX: Tu vero mimus mihi magis, quam naufragus
    Videre: tolle te hinc; aut ego mox omnia
    Quae reliqua habes, mecum auferam.
NAVEGUS: Nil mavelim:
    Nam mecum egestatem & famem circumfero,   660
    Quam quisquis auferat, volente me auferet.
DROPAX: Caeterum homo, tolle res tuas, & abi; jocis
    Venale nihil hic est.
NAVEGUS: Modo lacrimis siet?
DROPAX: Si seriae sint.
NAVEGUS: Atqui ego sum serius.
    Noctem unam in undis innatavi naufragus,   665
    Mortemque passus etiam antea, quam occumberem,
    Cum hoc remo ego evasi: reliqua venti, mare
    Rapuere cuncta. Juvate vos miserrimum
    Homuncionem.
DROPAX: Nostrae opis tibi per parum est.
    Sed in hac, vir unus omnium ditissimus   670
    Vicinia est, qui pauperes, ut liberos
    Suos fovet juvatque.

SMILAX: Who?
NAVEGUS: Starvation.
SMILAX: Starvation has no jurisdiction here.
NAVEGUS: I wish she hadn't. I'd like to leave the place.
SMILAX: She's no authority, and with impunity
    You can ignore her.
NAVEGUS: She herself has told me
    She rules here.
DROPAX: That was wrong. You had no need
    To trust her.
NAVEGUS: Well, she seemed so eloquent
    That she persuaded me.
DROPAX: We know the king to be
    Our ruler here.
NAVEGUS: Possibly. But Starvation
    Must be the queen.
SMILAX: I'll put her on the rack,
    This queen of yours.
NAVEGUS: Please do. She's giving me
    A racking time. My stomach's on the rack
    Because of her, and I can't make her leave.
SMILAX: You seem to be more clown than shipwrecked sailor.
    Take yourself off, or else I'll confiscate
    Everything you've got left.
NAVEGUS: I wouldn't mind.
    All that I carry round are want and hunger:
    I don't mind who takes *them* away from me!
DROPAX: Push off and take them with you, you can't buy
    A thing with jokes.
NAVEGUS: Only with tears, it seems?
DROPAX: Provided
    They're serious ones.
NAVEGUS: I'm serious enough. Shipwrecked,
    I spent a whole night swimming in the sea,
    Escaping half a hundred threatened deaths,
    Helped only by this oar. The winds and waves
    Devoured the rest. Please help a wretched man
    In time of need.
DROPAX: Our alms won't help you much.
    But an extremely rich man lives nearby
    Who helps and cherishes the poor as if
    They were his children.

NAVEGUS: Quod nomen viro?
DROPAX: Cenodoxus.
NAVEGUS: Itidem apud alios jam inaudij;
  Adibo, opemque flagitabo.
SMILAX: Sed cave
  Ut ne ostiatim ab urbe censum hunc exigas;   675
  Nam conditum est jam lustrum. Et est quinquennium
  Dum census imperetur alter.
NAVEGUS: Dabo operam.

SCENA VI
CENODOXUS, DAMA, NAVEGUS,
HYPOCRISIS, BRUNO, HUGO, EXORISTUS, PTOCHUS

CENODOXUS: Ubi venerint, huc tempori ad me adducito.
  Tenes?
DAMA: Probe.
NAVEGUS: Hic an ipsus est, quem quaerito?
  Adibo. Te per ego salutem ipsissimam   680
  Tuamque per virtutem, ut hanc miseram, precor,
  Miserere vitam.
HYPOCRISIS: Circumi prius oculis;
  Nemo uspiam est.
CENODOXUS: Apage.
NAVEGUS: Perij gemino malo,
  Terra marique: quorum & unum satis erat
  Nimisque perniciem in meam.   685
CENODOXUS: Silicernium,
  Apage. Perire te tua improbitas jubet:
  Undae tui ultrices sceleris in naufragum
  Saevire cogunt.
NAVEGUS: Ita tibi Numen pium
  Habeto; me quondam merentem credito
  Poenas dedisse; si meo merito impares,   690
  Nihil est, quod irascare; mitius solet
  Punire Numen, non ideo, ut immitius
  Homo in hominem desaeviat.
HYPOCRISIS: Sat impudens
  Rogator iste.
CENODOXUS: Hinc te sceleste extempulo

NAVEGUS: Named?

DROPAX: Named Cenodoxus.

NAVEGUS: So I've already heard. I'll go and beg
    For alms from him.

SMILAX: Don't go from door to door
    Exacting payment all around the town.
    You've struck the special tax time that comes round
    Every five years.

NAVEGUS: I'll do as you suggest.

SCENE VI

CENODOXUS, DAMA, NAVEGUS,

HYPOCRISY, BRUNO, HUGO, EXORISTUS, PTOCHUS

CENODOXUS: When they arrive show them straight in to me.
    Understand?

DAMA: Yes.

NAVEGUS: Is this the man I want?
    I'll try him. As you hope for your salvation,
    I beg you by your virtue to have pity
    On wretched me.

HYPOCRISY: First glance round. There's no-one
    Anywhere near.

CENODOXUS: Be off!

NAVEGUS: Two-fold disaster
    On land and sea assailed me: either one
    Enough to have finished me.

CENODOXUS: Out of my sight,
    You heap of bones. Your godless life has ruined you;
    The waves avenged your sins and shipwrecked you.

NAVEGUS: May God be gracious to you. I believe
    That I've deserved to suffer, and if now
    I suffer less than I deserve, that's nothing
    To anger you. If God is merciful
    It is not for the sake of making men
    Merciless to each other.

HYPOCRISY: Impudent
    Enough this beggar seems!

CENODOXUS: Get out of here,

Facesse: nulla dignus ope, si quem aequora   695
    Reum fatentur.
NAVEGUS: Ah tuae sortis memor,
    Miserare nostram. Olim pari clementia
    Faciet tui tibi gratiam piaculi
    Illud perenne Numen.
CENODOXUS: Improbum caput!
    Tu me tibi aequiparare? tun' piaculum   700
    Adscribere mihi? quem innocentem, & nullius
    Maleficij convincit orbis? quem sciunt
    Omnes benefaciendo, vitaeque inclytis
    Facinoribus vicisse cunctos? saeculis
    Probitatis exemplum futuris? hunc tui   705
    Similem, piaculis putes obnoxium?
    Ocyus abi, sceleste, maximam in malam
    Necem: periisti, denuo ubi te videro.
HYPOCRISIS: Hoc recte & ordine factum. Ubi nemo arbiter
    Virtutis est, ibi benefacere nil juvat.   710
NAVEGUS: Haeccine Viri illa tanta liberalitas?
    Haec illa beneficentia est? Superi, inferi
    Istos beneficos & benevolos perduint,
    A queis magis alapam petas, quam sportulam.
    Hic reculam nil est, quod augeat meam.   715
    Valete.
CENODOXUS: Bruno & Hugo veniunt denique.
    Salvete Bruno & Hugo.
BRUNO: Commodum adsumus
    Cenodoxe?
CENODOXUS: Nunquam incommodum: hic ego interim
    Solus vagabar, otia inter musica,
    Dum vos viderem.   720
HUGO: Te videre & colloqui
    Properavimus.
CENODOXUS: Ubi Lauduinus? ubi alij?
    Venire an abnuunt?
BRUNO: Sequuntur, brevi aderunt.
CENODOXUS: Placet intus opperirier. Subsellia
    Puer interim dispone, nostris ut siet
    Aptus locus sermocinationibus.   725
EXORISTUS: Te per tuam fortunam, & hocce caput tuum,
    Vir integerrime; miserere pauperum.

You rascal you. The waves proclaim your guilt;
                   You're worth no alms.
NAVEGUS: Be mindful of your lot,
                   And pity mine. Then everlasting God
                   With equal clemency will spare your sins
                   And give you grace.
CENODOXUS: You dare, you shameless wretch,
                   Compare yourself to me? Suggest that I
                   Have been a sinner, whom the world proclaims
                   Stainless and sinless? Who am known by all
                   To have won the hearts of men with my good works
                   And glorious deeds? My probity a model
                   For all posterity? You think this man
                   A sinner who is punishable like you?
                   You wretch! Get out! I'll have you put to death
                   If ever I set eyes on you again.
HYPOCRISY: Quite right and proper. Doing good is pointless
                   When there's no audience to approve your virtue.
NAVEGUS: Is this his marvellous generosity?
                   His kindness? Then may all the gods destroy
                   Benevolent and kind men such as this.
                   Instead of cash they'd rather box your ears.
                   I'll get no pittance here to ease my want.
                   Goodbye.
CENODOXUS: Here Bruno and Hugo come at last.
                   Greetings!
BRUNO: Do we disturb you, Cenodoxus?
CENODOXUS: Disturb me? Never! I was strolling here
                   Alone, relaxing with some music, waiting
                   Till I should see you.
HUGO: We have hurried here
                   To talk to you.
CENODOXUS: Laudwinus and the others,
                   Do they decline to come?
BRUNO: They're on their way,
                   And will be here quite soon.
CENODOXUS: Let's wait for them
                   Inside. And you, boy, go and set out chairs
                   So we can sit in comfort and converse.
EXORISTUS: By your good fortune, by your life, I beg
                   Your excellence to pity us poor men.

PTOCHUS: Barbarica passi vincula, longo carceris
Paedore torti, capite censi, quaerimus
Peculium, quo vindicemur.   730

EXORISTUS: Aspice
Squalentia situ membra; & in lucem assere
Quos diutina fames, atque nox exercuit.

HUGO: Absiste, ne molestus esto jam Viro.

EXORISTUS: Si absisteret ventris etiam molestia.

HYPOCRISIS: Vident; nihil morare, stips largissima   735
Largissimam tibi paritura est gloriam.

CENODOXUS: Absit molestus ut mihi sit quispiam
E plebe tenuium. Quibus vos vinculis
Dixistis attineri?

PTOCHUS: Ab hoste barbaro
Abhinc decennium ambo capti, patria   740
Simul occupata, liberis, uxoribus
Deperditis, in hosticam ducti sumus.

CENODOXUS: Hic singuli ternos habete Philippicos.
Memores mei, pro me subinde Numini
Supplicia fundite.   745

EXORISTUS, PTOCHUS: Te salus, amplissime
Vir, ipsa servet.

NAVEGUS: Non sacrificavi bonae
Fortunae, ut hodie mane surrexi: favet
Huic, mihi resistit. Aggredi denuo lubet,
Imo jubet esuritio. Solum tuis
Me arcebis a beneficijs? parce misero   750
Parique liberalitate me juva,
Ut distulisse me prius, non undique
Pepulisse videaris.

HYPOCRISIS: Age quod agis: plurimi
Tuentur; est dandum aliquid.

CENODOXUS: Ego te distuli,
Pepulive, mi homo?   755

NAVEGUS: Paulo ante.

CENODOXUS: Parcite Juvenes,
Haud scio rogasse.

NAVEGUS: Naufragus petij stipem
Paulo ante, & etiamnum peto.

BRUNO: Forte studijs
Intentus haud adverteras?

PTOCHUS: Squalid captivity and barbarous chains,
    Outlawed, we suffered long, and now seek alms
    To buy our freedom.
EXORISTUS: See our rotting limbs
    Covered with filth; bring back to light of day
    Men racked with famine and the dungeon's night.
HUGO: Desist now, do not trouble this great man.
EXORISTUS: Our stomachs should desist from troubling us.
HYPOCRISY: They're watching; don't delay, give bounteously;
    This will procure for you most bounteous glory.
CENODOXUS: Far be it from me to find the meanest man
    A trouble to me. But whose captive bonds
    Confined you?
PTOCHUS: Captured by a barbarous foe
    Ten years ago, our country occupied,
    Our wives and children lost, we both were led
    To spend a captive's life in foreign lands.
CENODOXUS: Here are three golden coins for each of you.
    Remember me and in your prayers to God
    Pray for me always.
EXORISTUS, PTOCHUS: May salvation's self
    Preserve you, Sir, most generous of men.
NAVEGUS: I didn't sacrifice, when I got up,
    To Lady Luck. She favours him, shuns me.
    Starvation eggs me on to beg again.
    Am I alone denied your alms? Have pity,
    Be just as generous to wretched me.
    Though you have put me off, don't let it seem
    You've totally denied me.
HYPOCRISY: You're being watched.
    Mind what you do and give him something.
CENODOXUS: I
    Denied, rejected you, my man?
NAVEGUS: Just now.
CENODOXUS: Forgive me, friends, I did not know he'd asked.
NAVEGUS: Shipwrecked, I asked for alms, and do again.
BRUNO: Immersed in thought, perhaps, you didn't notice?

CENODOXUS: Bono es animo,
    Pete; liberalem senties.
NAVEGUS: Quicquid dabit
    Tua liberalitas.   760
CENODOXUS: Philippaeos cape
    Duos.
NAVEGUS: DEUS te sospitet, vir maxime.
CENODOXUS: Amare pauperes, eosque primitus
    Curare didici.
HUGO: Liberalitas mihi
    Non visa major.
HYPOCRISIS: Hoc theatrum debuit
    Habere virtus.   765
CENODOXUS: Imus?
BRUNO: Ut tibi collubet.
NAVEGUS: Quanti interest, qua quis quid hora postulet?
    Ita homo repente mutat, ut qui heri Euclio
    Fuit, sub unam evadat horam prodigus.
    Chaldaeus essem, & astra talia noscerem,
    Paucis diebus a stipe ego ditescerem.   770

SCENA VII
PHILAUTIA

    Quid hoc? quid est quod sentio? rursus novis
    Acherunta concuti tumultibus? quid hoc?
    Iterumne custos carceris diri suis
    Trifaucia ora subrigit latratibus?
    An sede ab infausta! properat exercitus   775
    Plutonis omnis? imminet malum malis.
    Se tota vis infundit orbi. Sentio,
    Sentio: quatit Megaera crines noxios,
    Facesque Tisyphone cruenta ventilat;
    Cenodoxon omnes impetunt: omnes in hunc   780
    Sese inferunt. Video meas partes fore,
    Curare primas ut feram. Nunc cuditur
    Superba concertatio; qua caeteros
    Cenodoxus herbam sibi jubebit porgere,
    Ipse mihi solus porriget. Vincat alios   785
    Licet; nec evadet tamen victor mei
    Suique. Qui sic vincit alios, vincitur.

CENODOXUS: Take heart, and ask; you'll find me generous.
NAVEGUS: Whatever your generosity will give.
CENODOXUS: Here, take two sovereigns.
NAVEGUS: God preserve your grace.
CENODOXUS: I've learned above all else to love the poor
    And care for them.
HUGO: Such liberality
    I've never seen.
HYPOCRISY: Virtue deserves its place
    On such a stage.
CENODOXUS: We'll go then?
BRUNO: Certainly.
NAVEGUS: How much it matters, who asks what, and when!
    Men change so suddenly: yesterday's miser
    Today in one brief hour becomes a prodigal.
    I should tell fortunes, and take up astrology;
    In a few days of begging I'd get rich.

SCENE VII
SELF-LOVE

    What's this? What's this I feel? Is Acheron
    Shaken afresh with turbulence? What is it?
    Does that dire prison's warden stretch his heads
    Baying again from his tripartite throats?
    And from that ill-starred seat do all the hosts
    Of Pluto hasten forth? Ills pile on ills.
    Their total force engulfs the world. I see,
    I see Megaera shake her noxious locks,
    Bloody Tisyphone advance her firebrands;
    Their prey is Cenodoxus, all attack him.
    My first concern, then, is to be the spearhead
    Of this attack. The proud dispute is forged
    Where Cenodoxus, overriding all,
    Will claim submission; while himself submitting
    Only to me. All others he may conquer;
    Neither himself nor I shall vanquished be:
    Such vanquishers as he are their own victims.

SCENA VIII
DORUS, DROMUS, CLEPTES,
AESCULAPIUS, MACHAON

DROMUS: Tenete furem; hac hac profugit. Ocyus.
DORUS: Male sit malo capiti: tapetum nobile
    Me conspicante pene subripuit, scelus.   790
    Domo profugisse illum oportet primulum,
    Nec procul abisse.
DROMUS: Ego insequar prius, quam herus
    Revertat. Hac eo: Dore, tu illac quaerita.
AESCULAPIUS: Nihil afficit animum pari sensu meum
    Atque inter eruditioris seculi   795
    Juvenes virosque degere; atque illos modo
    Audire, modo rogare. Quo fit, ut nihil
    Hodieque praestabilius acciderit mihi,
    Quam more nostro disserentem attendere
    Cenodoxon.   800
MACHAON: Etsi juris ille peritiam
    Solum profiteatur, tamen alia omnia
    Tenet perinde docetque.
AESCULAPIUS: Nisi complurium
    Me cura febrientium discedere
    Jussisset, ibi adhuc essem; ita rapere me solet.
    Sed quis homo de meis pedem effert aedibus?   805
CLEPTES: Abisse me rebantur; Ego post januam
    Me absconderam. Nunc fugio demum tutius.
AESCULAPIUS: Heus tu, quid est operae tibi domi meae?
CLEPTES: Teneor miser furti. Quid habeo dicere?
AESCULAPIUS: Potin' ut mihi respondeas?   810
CLEPTES: Perij nimis.
    An tu vocaras?
AESCULAPIUS: Quid modo his tibi in aedibus?
CLEPTES: Mihi? ingredere tu, & sciscitare, quando ita
    Es curiosus.
AESCULAPIUS: Atqui ego hanc domum incolo.
    Jus est rogandi, quidnam apud meos agas?
CLEPTES: Dicam ergo. Nobile huc tapetum ex Belgio   815
    Venale porto: dictitant his aedibus
    Huic geminum haberi; tamque simile hoc alteri,
    Ovo est ut ovum. Proinde me operae credidi
    Facturum, ut huc afferrem, heroque ostenderem.

SCENE VIII
DORUS, DROMUS, CLEPTES,
AESCULAPIUS, MACHAON

DROMUS: Stop! I say stop thief! There he goes! Quick, quick!
DORUS: Damnation take him! Why, the rogue's made off
    With that expensive carpet while I watched him!
    He's only just this minute left the house,
    He can't be far away.
DROMUS: I'll go off after him
    Before the master's back. Go that way, Dorus.
AESCULAPIUS: There's nothing that affords me greater pleasure
    Than spending time with very learned men,
    The glory of our age, and listening to them,
    Asking them questions. Nothing's pleased me more
    Today than going to visit Cenodoxus,
    As we so often do, attending him,
    And listening to his talk.
MACHAON: And though he claims
    Only to know the law, he knows and teaches
    Everything else besides.
AESCULAPIUS: Had not a crowd
    Of ailing patients needed my attention,
    I'd still be there. Such is his hold on me.
    But who's this fellow coming from my house?
CLEPTES: They thought I'd got away, but I was hiding
    Behind the door. Now I can get out safely.
AESCULAPIUS: Here! You! What are you doing at my house?
CLEPTES: What am I going to say? I'm caught redhanded!
AESCULAPIUS: Well, can't you answer me?
CLEPTES: I've had it now!
    You called me, sir?
AESCULAPIUS: What are you doing here?
CLEPTES: Who, me? Go in and ask if you're so nosey.
AESCULAPIUS: But I'm the one who lives here. I've a right
    To ask you what you're doing in my house.
CLEPTES: I'll tell you then. This splendid Belgian carpet
    I'm offering for sale. They said its twin
    Was to be found here – both exactly similar
    Like as two peas. And so I thought I'd bring
    My carpet here and show it to the owner.

Sed herum negant adesse; tu si es, praestina.   820
MACHAON: Profecto, geminum est alteri, quod supra habes.
AESCULAPIUS: Quanti ergo vendis?
CLEPTES: Aureis numis eme
    Duobus & viginti.
AESCULAPIUS: Omittito duos;
    Viginti habebis.
CLEPTES: Egeo numis; caeterum haud
    Remitterem. At numera; morari non placet.   825
AESCULAPIUS: Numera Machaon. Saepe saepius fuit
    Mens, praestinare consimile, siquod foret.
    Nusquam antidhac reperire fuit: hic repperi.
CLEPTES: Discedo, gestis rebus ex sententia.
    Imo perij iterum. Est obviam, qui me puer   830
    In scelere manifesto tenuerat.
DORUS: Harpago,
    Suspendiarie; incidisti furcifer
    Meas manus. Ubi est tapes quem clepseras?
CLEPTES: St', mitte me: jam reddidi.
DORUS: Cui?
CLEPTES: Hero tuo.
    Omitte; jam placavi hominem: ibi; eccere; vides?   835
DORUS: Factum bene, alias nunquam omitterem: I, cave
    Redeas; peristi, simul ut iterum hic videro.
CLEPTES: Nunquam Lavernae sacrificavi equidem magis
    In tempore, ac hodie: in pedes nunc me dabo.
AESCULAPIUS: Dore ades, & hoc defer tapetum.   840
DORUS: Ut gaudeo
    Te hoc recuperasse, here; obsecro ubinam inveneras
    Hominem?
AESCULAPIUS: Ad fores meas.
DORUS: Et ego stupor merus,
    Tota urbe quaesij: ecquid erubuit trifur?
AESCULAPIUS: Cur erubesceret?
DORUS: Ita deprehensus.
AESCULAPIUS: Nihil.
DORUS: Eho, nihil? Ego me abdidissem in ultimos
    Mundi angulos.   845
AESCULAPIUS: Cur?
DORUS: Vapulavitne improbus?
AESCULAPIUS: Quid vapularet?

They say he's out. If you're the man, buy this.

MACHAON: Why, it's exactly like the one upstairs.

AESCULAPIUS: What do you want for it?

CLEPTES: Well, you can have it
For twenty-two pounds cash.

AESCULAPIUS: Knock off the two;
I'll give you twenty.

CLEPTES: Well, I'm short of cash–
And time–or else I wouldn't. Pay up, then.

AESCULAPIUS: Pay him, Machaon; it's what I've always wanted,
To buy another like it if I could.
I never saw another one till now.

CLEPTES: I'm off now. Things have gone extremely well.
Oh no! I'm done for once again. He's here–
The slave who caught me in the act.

DORUS: So now
I've got my hands on you, you thieving rogue.
Where did you put the carpet that you stole?

CLEPTES: Let go. I gave it back.

DORUS: Who to?

CLEPTES: Your boss.
Hands off. I've pacified him; look, I have.

DORUS: And just as well, or else you'd not escape me.
But don't come back, for if you do I'll get you.

CLEPTES: My offering to the patroness of thieves
Has never paid off better than today.
I'm off.

AESCULAPIUS: Come, Dorus, take this carpet in.

DORUS: I'm glad you've got it, sir. Where did you find him?

AESCULAPIUS: Here, by the door.

DORUS: And idiot I was searching
The whole town through. Did the wretch blush with shame?

AESCULAPIUS: Why should he?

DORUS: Caught like that!

AESCULAPIUS: Why, no.

DORUS: What, no?
I'd have gone scuttling to earth's furthest corners!

AESCULAPIUS: Why?

DORUS: Did he get a beating, then, the rogue?

AESCULAPIUS: Why should he?

DORUS: Saepe, here, nimis es bonus.
  Flagra meruit certe.
AESCULAPIUS: Imo meruit gratiam.
  Nam vile precium est, quod dedi. Tanto altero
  Pluris stat alterum.   850
DORUS: Quod illud alterum?
AESCULAPIUS: Quod supra habemus.
DORUS: Illud ipsum hoc est, here.
AESCULAPIUS: Hoc imo demum praestinavi.
DORUS: Falleris;
  Tuum erat inemtum.
AESCULAPIUS: Ain' meum tu? quomodo?
DORUS: Vae mihi! Nequij cavere: fur cubiculum
  Ingressus, illud abstulit.   855
AESCULAPIUS: Qui & vendidit
  Jam mihi?
DORUS: Ita.
AESCULAPIUS: Quicum collocutus es modo?
DORUS: Ita.
AESCULAPIUS: Quin tenebrionem ergo tenuisti hic, stupor?
DORUS: Tenebam: at ille reddidisse jam tibi
  Se dixit.
AESCULAPIUS: Ignavum caput: ego, ego tibi,
  Trifurcifer, reddam loco illius malum.   860
DORUS: Quid enim ego feci?
MACHAON: Tempera iram; innoxius
  Puer est.
AESCULAPIUS: Cavere debuit furis manus.
MACHAON: Et cavere furis debuisti tu dolos.
AESCULAPIUS: Uterque noxij sumus; sed magis ego.

DORUS: Sir, you're often far too kind.
    He really earned some blows.
AESCULAPIUS: He earned my thanks.
    I got it very cheap. The other one
    Cost twice as much.
DORUS: What other one?
AESCULAPIUS: The one
    We've got upstairs.
DORUS: But that one's this one, sir.
AESCULAPIUS: No, no, I've just bought this one.
DORUS: You're mistaken.
    It was yours before you bought it.
AESCULAPIUS: Mine you say?
    Why, how?
DORUS: Unhappily I couldn't stop it.
    The thief went in and stole it.
AESCULAPIUS: That man here
    Who sold it to me?
DORUS: Yes.
AESCULAPIUS: The one I spoke to?
DORUS: Yes.
AESCULAPIUS: Fool, why didn't you hold him?
DORUS: But I did.
    He said he'd given you the carpet back.
AESCULAPIUS: You worthless wretch, I'll make you pay his penalty
    And suffer in his place.
DORUS: What have I done?
MACHAON: Calm down, calm down; the lad is not to blame.
AESCULAPIUS: He should have been on guard and stopped the thief.
MACHAON: You should have been on guard against his tricks.
AESCULAPIUS: Then we are both to blame; I more than he.

SCENA IX
CENODOXUS, PHILAUTIA,
DAMA, RUSTICUS

CENODOXUS: Volupe est mihi, audire Juvenum haec encomia,
  Quibus solent identidem applaudere mihi.   865
  Subit tamen lubido scire, ecquid foris
  Plebeia de me turba sentiant?
PHILAUTIA: Potin'
  Dubitare? multa, mira, magna scilicet.
CENODOXUS: Placet experiri. Dama, tu istunc mihi Senem
  Adduce sis.   870
DAMA: Heus, siste paulisper Senex.
RUSTICUS: Victoriatis & teruntijs tribus.
DAMA: Sistere ego jussi.
RUSTICUS: Constitit pluris mihi.
DAMA: Non hoc rogavi. Sed jubet meus te herus
  Ad se venire paullulum.
RUSTICUS: Ex suburbio.
DAMA: Longe aliud.   875
RUSTICUS: Haud ita longe abest.
DAMA: Ad rem, Senex.
RUSTICUS: Cum egrederer, hora tertia haud dum sonuerat.
DAMA: Non hoc volo.
RUSTICUS: Lento gradu; nam sum senex.
DAMA: Men' ludis?
RUSTICUS: Ego studere lucris non volo.
  Parce admodum vivo.
DAMA: Quid hominis est hic senex?
  Aliud rogatur, & aliud refert mihi.   880
RUSTICUS: Toties modo attuli, minoris non dedi.
DAMA: An audit aegre?
RUSTICUS: Ubi in forum devenero,
  Non deerit emtor: Mitte si emtum nil cupis.
DAMA: Ad herum, ad herum venire te jussi meum.
RUSTICUS: Me? haud ceperam te prius. Ubi est herus? 885
DAMA: Hic adest.
CENODOXUS: Recede, Dama; solus hunc ego colloquar.
  Unde huc in urbem, mi senex?
RUSTICUS: Ex viculo.
CENODOXUS: Nostine cives urbis hujus Principes?

SCENE IX
CENODOXUS, SELF-LOVE,
DAMA, RUSTICUS

CENODOXUS: How I luxuriate in these nobles' praises,
     The continuous applause they shower on me.
     Yet I would gladly know what common men
     Think of me in the world outside.
SELF-LOVE: Why, many things,
     All marvellous and magnificent. Can you doubt it?
CENODOXUS: I'd like to know. Bring that old man here, Dama.
DAMA: Hey, you old man, come over here a minute.
RUSTICUS: Three pennies and three farthings is the price.
DAMA: I said come here.
RUSTICUS: It cost me more than that.
DAMA: I didn't ask you that. My master says
     You must come here a moment.
RUSTICUS: From the suburbs.
DAMA: That's far from the point.
RUSTICUS: No, it's not far.
DAMA: Look here!
RUSTICUS: When I set out, the clock had just struck three.
DAMA: I didn't ask that.
RUSTICUS: Being old, I'm slow.
DAMA: Is this a game?
RUSTICUS: I'm not too bothered with gain.
     I lead a frugal life.
DAMA: What's up with him?
     I ask him one thing, he replies another.
RUSTICUS: As I keep saying, I didn't give less.
DAMA: Is he
     Deaf?
RUSTICUS: Once in the market I'll find customers.
     So let me go, if you don't want to buy.
DAMA: I ordered you to come and see my master.
RUSTICUS: Me? I misheard you. Where's your master?
DAMA: Here.
CENODOXUS: Dama, step back. I'll talk to him alone.
     You came to town from where, my man?
RUSTICUS: A village.
CENODOXUS: And do you know the top men of this city?

RUSTICUS: Aliquos.

CENODOXUS: Quid in suburbio de illis, bene
    Secusve dictitatur?   890

RUSTICUS: Ut quisque est bonus
    Secusve.

CENODOXUS: Cenodoxum probantne an improbant?

RUSTICUS: Quem quaeso Cenodoxum?

CENODOXUS: Urbis inter principes
    Ferme omnium unum principem.

RUSTICUS: Nunquam audij,
    Quid hominis esset?

CENODOXUS: Eho, an ergo tu nihil
    De litterato illo audijsti?   895

RUSTICUS: Adeo nihil.

CENODOXUS: De principe, inquio, Cenodoxo?

RUSTICUS: Adeo nihil.

CENODOXUS: De singulari illo erudito?

RUSTICUS: Adeo nihil.

CENODOXUS: Quem totus orbis norit?

RUSTICUS: Ego pars utique sum
    Totius orbis; nec tamen novi.

CENODOXUS: Cedo,
    Saepe hanc in urbem commeasti?   900

RUSTICUS: Quotidie.

CENODOXUS: Nec de hoc tamen viro audijsti?

RUSTICUS: Adeo nihil.

CENODOXUS: Qui fit?

RUSTICUS: Ego nescio: caeterum hoc scio; nihil
    Audisse de Cenodoxo.

CENODOXUS: In illum omnes solent
    Intendere digitos?

RUSTICUS: Licet & intenderent
    Pugnos; ego tamen audijsse nil scio.   905

CENODOXUS: Quid si videres illum, an illum nosceres?

RUSTICUS: Si diceret sese esse, forte crederem.

PHILAUTIA: Omitte stultum, sat tibi est, si caeteri
    Te noverint.

CENODOXUS: Sed est cupido noscere
    Illum virum?   910

RUSTICUS: Profecto nulla.

RUSTICUS: A few.

CENODOXUS: What's said about them in the suburbs,
Good things or bad?

RUSTICUS: Good things or bad according
To what they're like.

CENODOXUS: Do they praise Cenodoxus?

RUSTICUS: Who's Cenodoxus, might I ask?

CENODOXUS: The chief
Of all the city's chiefest men.

RUSTICUS: Who's that?
I've never heard of him.

CENODOXUS: You've never heard
About his learning?

RUSTICUS: Never heard a thing.

CENODOXUS: That famous Cenodoxus?

RUSTICUS: Not a thing.

CENODOXUS: His marvellous erudition?

RUSTICUS: Not a thing.

CENODOXUS: Who's known the whole world over?

RUSTICUS: I'm a part
Of the whole world, and I don't know him.

CENODOXUS: Tell me,
Do you frequent this city often?

RUSTICUS: Daily.

CENODOXUS: And you've heard nothing of this man?

RUSTICUS: No, nothing.

CENODOXUS: Why's that?

RUSTICUS: I've no idea. But this I do know,
That I've heard nothing about Cenodoxus.

CENODOXUS: Everyone points to him.

RUSTICUS: They can all punch him
For all I care, but I've heard nothing of him.

CENODOXUS: What if you saw him, would you know him then?

RUSTICUS: I might believe him if he told his name.

SELF-LOVE: Ignore the fool, it's quite enough if others
Know about you.

CENODOXUS: And do you feel no wish
To know the man?

RUSTICUS: No, none.

CENODOXUS: Plurimi
        Precio emerent, ut eum viderent.
RUSTICUS: Mortui
        Fortasse, vel caeci. At ego si Teruntio
        Centum emere Cenodoxos queam, emere non velim.
        Sed ne morare me: forum abeo.
PHILAUTIA: Quam parum
        Novere Rustici.   915
CENODOXUS: Ruborem prope mihi
        Excussit istaec hominis ignoratio.
        Notum esse me autumabam ubique gentium;
        Nunc ne in suburbano quidem novere me.
PHILAUTIA: Nempe ista rusticana turba desipit.
        Nil est morandum, quid probet, quidve improbet!   920

CENODOXUS:　　　　　　　　Many would pay
　　Good money for a sight of him.
RUSTICUS:　　　　　　　　The dead
　　Or blind perhaps. I wouldn't give you tuppence
　　To buy a hundred Cenodoxuses.
　　Don't hold me up. I'm off to market.
SELF-LOVE:　　　　　　　　Rustics
　　Are very ignorant.
CENODOXUS:　　　　His ignorance
　　Has almost forced a blush into my cheeks.
　　I thought that I was known the whole world over;
　　Yet even in our suburbs I'm not known.
SELF-LOVE: That crowd of clodhoppers has got no sense.
　　Don't waste time on its likes or its dislikes!

ACTUS III

SCENA I
CENODOXOPHYLAX

Heu me; labores irritos; evanidam
Beneficiorum memoriam! Adsum denuo,
Ut ubi meam operam saepe lusi, ludere
Aggrediar ultimum. Bonus sum ego Genius
Cenodoxo; at ille me quasi malum exterminat.   925
Fugit, odit, exsecratur; heu male nescius
Properantis irae; nescius fati sui
Jam jam futuri; nescius periculi
Praesentis; & suae ruinae nescius.
Cenodoxe, satis est: ah satis superbiae   930
Datum est; satis Cenodoxe. Nunquam tu tui
Memor eris? arrogantiae nullum modum
Finemve pones? nulla tandem gloriae
Cupidinem dies tibi auferet? auferet;
Sed sero nimis: auferet. Ubi alijs proderis,   935
Oberis tibi: docebis alios vivere,
Peribis ipse. Scilicet magno voles
Hujus redemtam gloriae pruriginem;
Sapiesque cum resipiscere tibi negabitur.
Jam jam periisses, nisi meis tibi precibus   940
Moram impetrassem. At vereor ut frustra siem;
Et hinc recedam lusus, ut saepe anteidhac.
Tentabo tamen, & ultimo superbiam
Ariete verberabo.

Act Three

Alas; vain toil; of all my benefits
The memory is vanished. I return
To play the final throw where I have squandered
My pains so often. Cenodoxus spurns me
As if I were his Evil, not his Good.
He flees me, hates, reviles me – all too ignorant
Of the impending wrath and of his fate
Immediately imminent; unknowing
Of present danger and his own destruction.
Enough now, Cenodoxus, of your pride,
The limit's reached; enough now, Cenodoxus.
Have you no memory of your own true self?
Is there no limit to your boundless arrogance?
No final date to end your lust for glory?
There is: but much too late. In furthering others,
You'll fail yourself; yes, you yourself will perish
In teaching others life. How you will wish
The lust for this vain glory were atoned for.
You will be wise, when wisdom's way is barred.
You would be lost already, had not my prayers
Gained you respite. I fear I toil in vain
And shall retreat the loser, as before.
I shall attempt it, though, and on his pride
Make one last, battering assault.

SCENA II
CENODOXUS, MARISCUS,
CENODOXOPHYLAX, PANURGUS

CENODOXUS: Dudum nescio
     Quid ordiar; non edere, non bibere juvat:
     Nec lectio mihi nauseam, nec scriptio   945
     Eximit.
MARISCUS: Id esse mirum in his negotijs,
     Cenodoxe? diripiunt prope omnes te, tua
     Orbis ope sustentatur: incumbit humeris
     Tuis onus, quod ferre nequeat Atlas suis.   950
CENODOXUS: Gravantur alto fessa somno lumina.
     Non pugno: membra do quieti. Hinc tu interim
     Abi; Nec interpellet alius quispiam
     Meam quietem.
MARISCUS: Aegre mihi est, quoties dolet
     Cenodoxus. Illum, ut coenitem, praeconijs   955
     Extollo: quem laudare cum nequeo, simul
     Coenare nequeo.
CENODOXOPHYLAX: A me revincta lumina
     Sunt hoc sopore: insomnijs terrebitur,
     Quem saepe vigilem aggressus haud quicquam fui.
     Cenodoxe, commigrabis: ultimum hoc tuae   960
     Spatium diei est. Caeterum ratio tibi est
     Ducenda. Contuere, quid libri feram?
     Hic lege. Quid horres facinora tua! Serus es;
     Horrere dudum oportuit. Viden' tuas
     Offucias? viden' apinas? Mortalibus   965
     Os sublinere licebat; immortalibus
     Fumum facere fucumque, non est. Num vides
     Superbiam? superbiam? superbiam?
     Si centies legas, superbiam leges;
     Si millies legas, superbiam leges;   970
     Deciesque centiesque millies leges.
     Agnoscis?
CENODOXUS: Ah ah ah!
CENODOXOPHYLAX: Migrabimus.
CENODOXUS: Moram.
CENODOXOPHYLAX: Nihil agis; evocaberis. Panurge, ades
     Cohorte cum socia inferis e sedibus.

SCENE II
CENODOXUS, MARISCUS,
CENODOXOPHYLAX, PANURGUS

CENODOXUS: I'm lost
  These days past. Neither food nor drink delights me,
  Nor if I read or write does this relieve
  My nausea.
MARISCUS: With your worries, Cenodoxus,
  Are you surprised? You're almost torn apart
  By everybody; you support the world,
  Shouldering a burden Atlas could not carry.
CENODOXUS: A heavy slumber strains my weary eyes.
  I'll not resist it; let me rest my limbs
  A while; and let nobody else disturb
  My rest.
MARISCUS: When Cenodoxus is not well
  I suffer too. I shower him with praise
  To earn a meal; and when I can't extol him,
  Then I can't dine.
CENODOXOPHYLAX: It's I who've closed his eyes
  With sleep. He shall be terrified through dreams
  Whom waking I have often urged in vain.
  You must depart, Cenodoxus. This one day
  Completes your span of life. Your reckoning
  Must be drawn up. You see the book I bear?
  Read here. You shudder at your crimes? It's late.
  You should have shuddered long ago. Do you
  Behold your wiles, your tricks? You may hoodwink
  Mere mortals; but you cannot fool or trick
  Almighty God. Do you not see your pride?
  Your pride, I say, your pride? If you should read
  A hundred times, it will be pride you read;
  A thousand times, a hundred thousand times,
  And still it will be pride. Do you perceive this?
CENODOXUS: Ah, ah!
CENODOXOPHYLAX: We must depart.
CENODOXUS: Delay a while.
CENODOXOPHYLAX: In vain. You shall be summoned forth. Panurgus,
  Abandon Hell and come here with your throng.

PANURGUS: Quis evocat?   975
CENODOXOPHYLAX: Suprema virtus Numinis.
PANURGUS: Quid imperat?
CENODOXOPHYLAX: Terrere Cenodoxum jubet.
PANURGUS: Resipiscet inde.
CENODOXOPHYLAX: Utinam quidem.
PANURGUS: Nolo.
CENODOXOPHYLAX: Volo.
     Jubeo, impero.
PANURGUS: Terrebone meos?
CENODOXOPHYLAX: Impero
     Sceleste; parendum est.
PANURGUS: Necabo igitur.
CENODOXOPHYLAX: Veto
     Necare; caeterum volo terrefieri.   980
     Accede; nec desiste, donec reveniam.

SCENA III
PANURGUS, CENODOXUS, ASTEROTH,
ASEMPHOLOTH, CENODOXOPHYLAX

PANURGUS: Quae praeda mihi devota? jam nunc faucibus
     Erebi inferenda? ubi est? ubi est? video. Asteroth,
     Asempholoth, venite praedam tollite.
CENODOXUS: Miserere; parce.   985
ASTEROTH: Quo vocamur?
PANURGUS: Huc mei
     Pars fida gregis.
ASEMPHOLOTH: An ducimus, rapimus scelus?
ASTEROTH: Age, evome animum sceleribus magnis, novis,
     Multis, gravibus obnoxium.
CENODOXUS: Ah, ah, ah! moram,
     Moram.
PANURGUS: Negamus.
ASTEROTH: Tu moram improbe flagites?
     Dudum trahendus & dicandus Tartaro.   990
ASEMPHOLOTH: Fauces nocentes, & nocentem spiritum
     Elido sceleri.
CENODOXUS: Heu, heu, juvate.
PANURGUS: Quis juvet?
     Noster es, erisque: ducite, trahite, rapite.

PANURGUS: Who summons me?
CENODOXOPHYLAX: God's mighty majesty.
PANURGUS: And His command?
CENODOXOPHYLAX: To frighten Cenodoxus.
PANURGUS: Then he'll repent!
CENODOXOPHYLAX: I wish he would!
PANURGUS: No, no!
CENODOXOPHYLAX: You must, I order it.
PANURGUS: Affright my prey?
CENODOXOPHYLAX: You must obey my bidding.
PANURGUS: Then I'll kill him.
CENODOXOPHYLAX: That I forbid. I want him filled with terror.
      Go to it; do not cease till I return.

SCENE III
PANURGUS, CENODOXUS, ASTEROTH,
ASEMPHOLOTH, CENODOXOPHYLAX

PANURGUS: What prey is mine? Now destined for the jaws
    Of Erebus? Where is it? Asteroth,
    Asempholoth, bear off the prey I see.
CENODOXUS: Have pity, spare me.
ASTEROTH: Where are we summoned?
PANURGUS: Here,
    My faithful throng.
ASEMPHOLOTH: Are we to seize this sinner?
ASTEROTH: Spew up your soul guilt-laden with vast crimes,
    Many and new.
CENODOXUS: Ah, wait a while, delay.
PANURGUS: We won't.
ASTEROTH: You beg for time, you shameless wretch?
    Marked down for long to be dragged off to Hell!
ASEMPHOLOTH: I'll seize his guilty throat and throttle out
    His guilty breath.
CENODOXUS: Ah, help me!
PANURGUS: Who can help?
    You're ours, for good; seize, rend him, bear him off.

CENODOXUS: Superi!

ASTEROTH: Inferi sumus: vocari nos decet.

CENODOXUS: Date spatium, heu!   995

PANURGUS: Apud nos spatium erit.

ASEMPHOLOTH: Nimis moramur, noster est.

ASTEROTH: Praelusimus
  Diu satis; rapiendus est. Hos mihi pedes.

ASEMPHOLOTH: Has ego manus mihi destino.

PANURGUS: Animum Tartaro.

CENODOXUS: DEUS eripe.

PANURGUS: Deum cogitas? Non ille te.

ASTEROTH: Tumet tibi fueras DEUS, te appellita.   1000

CENODOXUS: Succurre Numen.

ASEMPHOLOTH: Frustra es; odit, negligit,
  Contemnit, ut tu Numen hactenus.

CENODOXUS: At ego
  Nunquam Tonantem spreveram.

PANURGUS: Superbiam
  Non spreveras, & arrogantiam tuam.

ASEMPHOLOTH: Oggannit etiam? ad latera lamnas admove   1005
  Facesque.

PANURGUS: Nostra supplicia jam sentiat,
  Aequare qui nostram ausus est superbiam.

ASTEROTH: Imo superare.

CENODOXUS: Christe, postremam manum
  Porge misero.

ASEMPHOLOTH: Jam audire tandem vis miser?
  Esse potes; hoc datur.   1010

PANURGUS: Prope absumus: praei
  Aliquis, & Orcum pande.

CENODOXUS: Caelites mihi
  Omnes adeste; vimque prohibete inferae
  Cohortis.

PANURGUS: Aderunt, & juvabunt te Stygi
  Immergere.

ASTEROTH: Hic tandem adsumus propter specus
  Horrentis Erebi: hac mergite feram.   1015

CENODOXUS: Oh heavenly hosts!

ASTEROTH: We're hellish hosts; it's us
    You should invoke.

CENODOXUS: Give me a little time!

PANURGUS: You'll have a lot of time with us.

ASEMPHOLOTH: Don't wait;
    He's ours.

ASTEROTH: We've played too long. Let's haul him off
    By the feet...

ASEMPHOLOTH: And hands.

PANURGUS: His soul is bound for Hell.

CENODOXUS: Oh save me, God!

PANURGUS: What, God? He'll not save you.

ASTEROTH: You were your own God, call upon yourself!

CENODOXUS: Help me, oh God!

ASEMPHOLOTH: No use. God hates, neglects,
    Despises you as you did him.

CENODOXUS: But I
    Have never spurned almighty God.

PANURGUS: Your pride,
    Your arrogance you have not spurned.

ASEMPHOLOTH: Is he
    Still muttering? Put red-hot irons and torches
    Against his sides.

PANURGUS: Hell's torture let him feel,
    Who dared to vie with us in pride.

ASTEROTH: Surpass
    Our pride, you mean.

CENODOXUS: Succour, oh Christ, this once
    My wretched state.

ASEMPHOLOTH: You want at last to hear
    Yourself deemed wretched? Right. We'll grant that.

PANURGUS: Go;
    We're approaching Hell, lay Orcus open.

CENODOXUS: Angels
    Attend me, pit your strength against the hordes
    Of Hell.

PANURGUS: They'll come and help to plunge you deep
    Into the Styx. ,

ASTEROTH: At last we near the caverns
    Of fearful Erebus; here plunge him in.

ASEMPHOLOTH: Trudite,
     Pellite. Patet aditus inferorum. Sentio
     Luctantis horridum camini incendium.
     Immittite feram.
ASTEROTH: Assetur; & Laconicum.
     Nostrum pati assuefiat.
CENODOXUS: Heu, heu, quem mihi
     Quaero advocatum? Tu ales, o rebus meis   1020
     Spes una; propera.
CENODOXOPHYLAX: Quo vocas?
CENODOXUS: Me perditum
     Ut eruas.
CENODOXOPHYLAX: Ten' eruam? non audio;
     Audire quem nunquam volebas.
CENODOXUS: Audiam
     De caetero.
PANURGUS: Nihil agit; hoc timor exprimit.
     Ubi rursus in tutum redierit, ad suum   1025
     Redibit ingenium.
ASTEROTH: Fidem superbia
     Servare nescit.
CENODOXUS: Recipio sancte.
ASEMPHOLOTH: Nihil
     In homine sanctum est improbo: Nihil.
CENODOXOPHYLAX: Vale,
     Cenodoxe.
CENODOXUS: Serva miserum.
CENODOXOPHYLAX: Ubi te esse miserum
     Credideris.
CENODOXUS: Esse credo.   1030
PANURGUS: Non credit, scelus:
     Imponit.
CENODOXOPHYLAX: Hinc facesse jam stygia manus,
     Mox avola, praedamque mitte.
ASTEROTH: Superbior
     Nobis scelestiorque lucem hanc occupet,
     Qua nos jubemur cedere?
CENODOXOPHYLAX: Ocyus fuge.
     In gratiam recipio alumnum.   1035
ASEMPHOLOTH: Gratia
     Mox excidet.

ASEMPHOLOTH: Impel and drive him on. Hell's door yawns open.
    I feel the oven's fires and sulphurous flames.
    Dispatch the beast.

ASTEROTH: And let him roast and sweat,
    And learn to bear our tortures.

CENODOXUS: Ah! What advocate
    Shall plead for me? Good angel, my one hope,
    Come quickly.

CENODOXOPHYLAX: Where? Who calls?

CENODOXUS: Ah! Save me! Save me!
    I'm lost!

CENODOXOPHYLAX: Save you? I cannot hear you, you
    Who never wished to hear me.

CENODOXUS   I will hear
    From henceforth.

PANURGUS: No, he won't. It's fear says this.
    When he's restored to safety, he'll revert
    To his old ways.

ASTEROTH: His pride cannot keep faith.

CENODOXUS: I vow by all that's holy…

ASEMPHOLOTH: Nothing's holy
    About that vile wretch.

CENODOXOPHYLAX: Farewell, Cenodoxus.

CENODOXUS: Save miserable me.

CENODOXOPHYLAX: If you do truly
    Believe you're miserable.

CENODOXUS: I do.

PANURGUS: Don't trust him.
    This is deceit.

CENODOXOPHYLAX: Depart, you hosts of Hell,
    Go now, release your prey.

ASTEROTH: The man surpassing
    Our pride and crimes is to enjoy the light,
    And we are told to go?

CENODOXOPHYLAX: Yes, speed your flight,
    For I restore my ward to grace.

ASEMPHOLOTH: To grace
    He'll soon be lost.

CENODOXOPHYLAX: Tunc nil vetabo.

ASTEROTH: Noster est.

CENODOXOPHYLAX: Nondum est.

PANURGUS: Erit.

CENODOXOPHYLAX: Deus hoc cavebit: caeterum
    Nondum est. Fugam capessite.

CENODOXUS: Heu, quid debeo
    Tibi liberator?

CENODOXOPHYLAX: Hanc superbiam mihi
    Debes: relinque fastum; habere non potes   1040
    Mentis superbae sensa, si vel me voles
    Habere, vel DEUM; imo si te etiam voles.
    Absiste coeptis: & periculi memor
    Praesentis, a futuro abesse cogita.

SCENA IV

CENODOXUS, PHILAUTIA

CENODOXUS: Ludorne, mihi superstes ipse? mortuus   1045
    An vivo? vivusne morior? Neutrum; an simul
    Utrumque vere senseram? Quis me metus
    Versabat? etiamnum trepido. Quiescere
    Occoeperam; imo non quiescere, Superi!
    Sed aestuare, sed periclitarier   1050
    Vita atque capite. Quis etenim Proserpinae
    Furvae adierat regna, & tribunal Aeaci
    Propius? hiabat orcus in meum caput:
    Trahebat, impellebat undique carnifex
    Non unus: adeo uti meam precario   1055
    Redemerim vitam ac salutem. Eheu, nefas!
    Adeone sum improbus? adeone sceleribus
    Oppressus omnibus, merear ut Tartara?

PHILAUTIA: Caelum mereris.

CENODOXUS: Ambigere somnus jubet.

PHILAUTIA: Ambigere veritas vetat.   1060

CENODOXUS: Periculum
    Me terruit.

PHILAUTIA: Quod esse virtuti queat
    Periculum?

CENODOXUS: Quod ante paululum adieram.

CENODOXOPHYLAX: I'll then deny you nothing.

ASTEROTH: He's ours.

CENODOXOPHYLAX: Not yet.

PANURGUS: He will be.

CENODOXOPHYLAX: God forbid;
    He's not yours yet. Now go.

CENODOXUS: How much I owe
    To you, my rescuer!

CENODOXOPHYLAX: Your debt is pride:
    Cast off your arrogance. You cannot have
    A mind possessed by pride if you would have
    Your God, or me, or even your own self.
    Abandon these your sins; and mindful of
    Your present peril, keep future harm at bay.

SCENE IV

CENODOXUS, SELF-LOVE

CENODOXUS: Am I deluded? Do I live or die?
    Or die a living death? Do I feel both
    Or neither to be true? What fear possessed me?
    I'm trembling even now. I had begun
    To rest myself – that was no rest, oh God!
    I burned within and stood in mortal peril
    To life and soul. Who then but I approached
    Dark Proserpina's realms and the judgement-seat
    Of Aeacus? Hell gaped wide-jawed before me;
    Tormenting fiends attacked me from all sides
    And dragged me on; and I scarce gained salvation
    And life through my entreaties. Ah! Am I
    So reprobate, so steeped in every crime,
    That I deserve to be cast down to hell?

SELF-LOVE: You merit Heaven.

CENODOXUS: This my dream makes doubtful.

SELF-LOVE: The truth removes all doubt.

CENODOXUS: And yet the peril
    Has terrified me.

SELF-LOVE: What peril can afflict
    Your virtue?

CENODOXUS: That which I've now been exposed to.

PHILAUTIA: Somnia fuere, non pericula.

CENODOXUS: Et tamen
    Metuenda.

PHILAUTIA: Pueris.

CENODOXUS: Saepe vera somniant
    Sapientiores.   1065

PHILAUTIA: Vana falsaque saepius.

CENODOXUS: Quid haec fuisse certa prohibet?

PHILAUTIA: Quid eadem
    Fuisse inania vetat?

CENODOXUS: Atqui senseram
    Memet periclitari!

PHILAUTIA: Ita esse, somnium
    Suadebat.

CENODOXUS: Heu quam tetra mihi, quamque horrida
    Cacodaemonum occursabat acies?   1070

PHILAUTIA: Tu magis
    Horrendus ipsis.

CENODOXUS: Vindicare in crimina
    Mea appetebant.

PHILAUTIA: Imo virtutis odio
    Te prosecuti.

CENODOXUS: Non solent virtutibus
    Ita minitari.

PHILAUTIA: An nescius es, Antonios
    Olim, Macariosque, eorundem impetus   1075
    Tulisse, sanctimoniae laude inclytos?
    Nam sanctitas est, quae improbatur improbis.
    An itaque nescis, quae tua erga pauperes
    Sit liberalitas?

CENODOXUS: Scio equidem.

PHILAUTIA: Charitas
    Adversus infimos?   1080

CENODOXUS: Scio.

PHILAUTIA: Patientia
    In consulentes?

CENODOXUS: Scio.

PHILAUTIA: Dein' modestia
    In prosperis?

CENODOXUS: Scio.

PHILAUTIA: Dein' constantia
    In tristibus?

SELF-LOVE: They were mere dreams, not perils.

CENODOXUS: They exact
   Their toll of fear.

SELF-LOVE: From boys perhaps.

CENODOXUS: Wise men
   Have true dreams often.

SELF-LOVE: False ones more often still.

CENODOXUS: Why should I not believe it true?

SELF-LOVE: Why not
   Believe your dream was vain?

CENODOXUS: And yet I felt
   The danger threatening me.

SELF-LOVE: That was your dream
   Deluding you.

CENODOXUS: How foul the host of devils
   Assaulting me, how terrifying!

SELF-LOVE: You
   Terrified them much more.

CENODOXUS: They sought revenge
   On all my crimes.

SELF-LOVE: Their hatred of your virtue
   Made them torment you.

CENODOXUS: Virtues are not usually
   So threatened.

SELF-LOVE: Yet both Antony and Macarius
   Withstood the assaults of Hell and are renowned
   For sanctity – have you forgotten this?
   For sanctity is always reprobated
   By reprobates. Think of your liberality
   Towards the poor?

CENODOXUS: I know.

SELF-LOVE: Your charity
   Towards the oppressed?

CENODOXUS: I know.

SELF-LOVE: The patient way
   You give advice?

CENODOXUS: I know.

SELF-LOVE: Your modesty
   Despite success?

CENODOXUS: I know.

SELF-LOVE: Your constancy
   In all adversity?

CENODOXUS: Scio.
PHILAUTIA: Post, continentia
    Quanta?
CENODOXUS: Scio.
PHILAUTIA: Post, quanta abstinentia tibi sit?
CENODOXUS: Scio.   1085
PHILAUTIA: Post, precandi assiduitas?
CENODOXUS: Scio.
PHILAUTIA: Postmodum
    Quanta pietas erga DEUM?
CENODOXUS: Scio talia;
    Tamen!
PHILAUTIA: Quid hic? Virtutibus veris via
    Ad sidera impervia? Injustus DEUS
    Et iniquus est, si ferre tam injusta poterit.
CENODOXUS: Metuo tamen, metuo miser.   1090

SCENA V
MARISCUS, PHILAUTIA, CENODOXUS

MARISCUS: Dormitne adhuc?
    Vigilat. Sed est subtristis.
PHILAUTIA: Obliviscere
    Inane somnium.
CENODOXUS: Si inane somnium
    Foret.
PHILAUTIA: Est inane.
CENODOXUS: Sit utinam!
MARISCUS: Secum actitat
    Nescio quid occulti. Occupavero prior.
    Cenodoxe, ut ego suspenso adambulans gradu   1095
    Horsum tetendi, ne acquiescentem meo
    Strepitu moverem.
CENODOXUS: Veneras maturius;
    Nunquam minus meridiantem inveneras.
    Quies, an inquies mage fuerit, nescio,
    Quam capere cogitaveram.   1100
MARISCUS: Quid enim mali
    Turbavit?
CENODOXUS: Horribilia spectra in somnijs.

CENODOXUS: I know.
SELF-LOVE: Your continence?
CENODOXUS: I know.
SELF-LOVE: And your great abstinence?
CENODOXUS: I know.
SELF-LOVE: Your constant prayers?
CENODOXUS: I know.
SELF-LOVE: What piety
    You show towards God?
CENODOXUS: I know all this; and yet!
SELF-LOVE: What then? The road to glory shall be barred
    To your true virtues? God must be unjust,
    Inimical, to sanction such injustice.
CENODOXUS: Yet I'm afraid, afraid.

SCENE V
MARISCUS, SELF-LOVE, CENODOXUS

MARISCUS: Is he still sleeping?
    Awake, but somewhat sad.
SELF-LOVE: Empty your mind
    Of this vain dream.
CENODOXUS: If only it were vain.
SELF-LOVE: It is.
CENODOXUS: I wish it were.
MARISCUS: He's brooding on
    Some hidden thought. I'll greet him. Cenodoxus,
    I've made my way here almost on tiptoe
    Lest I should make a noise and so disturb you
    When you were resting.
CENODOXUS: Would you had come here sooner!
    Never would you have come to one less restful.
    I hardly know if it was rest or unrest
    That had the upper hand.
MARISCUS: What ill disturbed
    Your rest?
CENODOXUS: Some fearful visions in my dreams.

MARISCUS: Ho ho; redi ad Hilaria; absque causa tristis es.
    Quae somnijs fides?

CENODOXUS: Subinde plurima.

MARISCUS: Subinde nulla.

CENODOXUS: Vereor ut hodie siet
    Aliqua!   1105

MARISCUS: Nihil. Hodie esse nullam credito:
    Cras senties secus, ubi somniaveris
    Meliora.

CENODOXUS: Quid ita?

MARISCUS: Doctus ego sum; calleo
    Mathesin. Hodie portam eburneam Sopor
    Ingressus, ulmum ventilaverat manu.
    Proinde vanum est, quicquid hodie suggerit.   1110

CENODOXUS: Suggessit etiam te esse mecum in coenula.

MARISCUS: Hic vera suggessit, quia & cras suggeret.

CENODOXUS: Cras somniare nolo.

MARISCUS: Somnia, si sapis;
    Nam corneas redibit ad fores sopor,
    Ni astrologica fallor fide: tunc lucida,   1115
    Tunc vera, tunc jucunda venient somnia.

CENODOXUS: Quo vate didicisti hoc?

MARISCUS: Egomet enim mihi
    Soleo esse vates, quandocunque scilicet
    Bissexto in anno, mense Januario,
    Hebdomade septima, dies Veneris, diem   1120
    Jovis praeit.

CENODOXUS: Tu vero nugo totus es.

MARISCUS: Qui somnia audis, me quoque audi: par fides
    Utrisque convenit. Sed an abeo, & tibi
    Coenam instruo Cenodoxe?

CENODOXUS: Quid hodie juvet
    Coenare?   1125

MARISCUS: Quid juvet? videbis: qui modo
    Ventrem habeo vacuum, habebo plenum postea.
    Hoc tu nihil putas juvare?

CENODOXUS: Sed mihi
    Coenare non lubet.

MARISCUS: Lubet vero mihi.
    Spectante te esitabo. Plane prosperum
    Hunc mihi diem, quo mensa tanti me viri   1130

MARISCUS: Ho, ho, cheer up. You've no cause to be sad.
    What trust is there in dreams?
CENODOXUS: Often a lot,
MARISCUS: And often none.
CENODOXUS: Today I feel there may
    Be some.
MARISCUS: Nonsense. I'm sure there's none today.
    Tomorrow, when your dreams will have been better,
    You'll feel quite different.
CENODOXUS: Why?
MARISCUS: Astrology
    I'm expert in. Sleep used the ivory door
    Today, and came in brandishing an elm.
    So all today's suggested dreams are idle.
CENODOXUS: It also made me dream you were my guest.
MARISCUS: That's true, because you'll dream the same tomorrow.
CENODOXUS: Tomorrow I'll not dream.
MARISCUS: Dream, if you're wise.
    Sleep will come through the horny doors again,
    Unless I read the stars amiss. The dreams
    You dream will be delightful, bright and true.
CENODOXUS: What oracle taught you that?
MARISCUS: I make a point
    Of being a seer whenever leap year comes,
    When January has seven whole weeks, and when
    Instead of Thursday, Friday comes before.
CENODOXUS: You're just a clown and nothing else.
MARISCUS: If you
    Take note of dreams, take note of me as well.
    Both can be trusted equally. I'll order
    Some dinner for you, shall I, Cenodoxus?
CENODOXUS: Why dine today?
MARISCUS: Why dine? See here–quite simply
    To fill the vacuum in my empty stomach.
    Isn't this reason good enough?
CENODOXUS: But I
    Don't want to dine.
MARISCUS: I want to very much.
    I'll eat and you can watch. How fortunate
    A day for me, when at this great man's table

    Dignabitur! alij quod optant, assequar
    Ego solus.
CENODOXUS: Ecquid illud, omnes quod vovent,
    Tu consequeris?
MARISCUS: Ut tibi conviva sim
    Frequentior, fruarque sermone aureo
    Avidissime.   1135
CENODOXUS: Licet: praei. Pellam hospite
    Jucundiore somnium teterrimum.

SCENA VI
MORBUS

    Nemo me adeo miretur aegre incedere,
    Cum morbus ego sim: hinc est, quod genua labant, manus
    Pectusque languent, ora pallent: viribus
    Destituor ipse, & destituo alios. Satis   1140
    Plerique jam nostis me, opinor; caeteri
    Noscetis olim. Huc mitto hodie ab alite
    Cenodoxophylace; faciam ut impetum in virum,
    Quem vidi ego aut novi hactenus nunquam: tamen
    Scio Cenodoxon esse; cui frustra fuit   1145
    Immissa nuper Conscientia: quem dein
    Metuenda frangere nequierunt somnia.
    Nunc denique mihi negotium datum est. Nihil
    Recuso: facile aedes & hominem reperiam,
    Eumque simul ac videro, invadam. Nam ita   1150
    Praecepit ales: tergiversari haud licet.

SCENA VII
PHILEDEMON, PHILARETUS, DAMA

PHILEDEMON: Hoc noctis ergo, Philarete, istuc accidit?
PHILARETUS: Haud aliud.
PHILEDEMON: Ipse videras?
PHILARETUS: Oculis meis.
PHILEDEMON: Quid audio?
PHILARETUS: Id quodvideram. Primitus enim
    Caliginem densissimam coegerant   1155

          I sit in state! What everyone would wish
          I can achieve alone.
CENODOXUS: What do all wish
          That you attain alone?
MARISCUS: To be your guest
          So often and enjoy your golden speech
          So avidly.
CENODOXUS: Well then; go in. Let's hope
          Gay company will dispel my fearful dreams.

SCENE VI
SICKNESS

          Let no-one marvel at my ailing entrance,
          For I am Sickness; hence my tottering limbs,
          My failing strength, my pallid face. Myself
          Bereft of power, others I bereave.
          Most of you know me well enough already,
          The rest will very soon. Today I'm sent
          By Cenodoxophylax to attack a man
          I've neither seen nor known till now: at least
          I know he's Cenodoxus, who in vain
          Was visited by Conscience recently,
          Whom even fearful nightmares could not break.
          At last the matter's put into my hands.
          I'll not demur. I'll find his house and him,
          And then attack immediately I see him.
          It's not for me to cavil at heaven's command.

SCENE VII
PHILEDEMON, PHILARETUS, DAMA

PHILEDEMON: You say it happened tonight, Philaretus?
PHILARETUS: It did.
PHILEDEMON: You saw it?
PHILARETUS: Yes, with my own eyes.
PHILEDEMON: Such things?
PHILARETUS: Yes, that I saw myself. At first
          Clouds formed in dense, impenetrable gloom,

Nubes; nec astra reliqua, praeter Cynthiam
Texere; Noctiluca tum forte fuerat.
Huic se illa tetra, horrenda, formidabilis
Opposuit umbra; sustulitque funditus
Mortalium conspectu.   1160

PHILEDEMON: Nihildum insolens.

PHILARETUS: Hinc fulgurare, ardere, stridere; quatere,
Turbare coelum. Frigidus mihi pectora
Pervasit horror: illico apparent novae
Facies, & ora ipsis timenda Manibus.
Deinde fremitus colloquentium, & minae   1165
Jactantur; intellecta nemini.

PHILEDEMON: Vigil
An somnians spectaveras?

PHILARETUS: Nil certius,
Vigilem fuisse.

PHILEDEMON: Quid dehinc?

PHILARETUS: Unus aliquis
Altum istud inclamare visus est mihi:
Properemus. Omnes inde fulminis in modum   1170
Terram institerunt petere: Nec vero hinc procul
Residere. Territus & prope examinus meos
Memet recepi ad familiares. Hinc simul
Ex commodo possem, apparabam accedere
Cenodoxon; illique mea visa exponere.   1175

PHILEDEMON: Comitabor; audiamque quidnam sentiat
Cenodoxus hoc tuo super miraculo,
Quem nunquam ego audij loquentem sine novo
Miraculo. Verum ecce, quo Dama properat?

PHILARETUS: Quid, puer, anhelas?   1180

DAMA: Mitte.

PHILARETUS: Siste.

DAMA: Non licet.
Properato opus.

PHILEDEMON: An est otiosus Herus?

DAMA: Herus?

PHILEDEMON: Herus, inquio; quem convenire collubet.

DAMA: Ah, herus. Omitte.

PHILEDEMON: Tergiversaris, puer?

DAMA: Absolve, quaeso.

PHILEDEMON: Non priusquam dixeris.

And covered every star; only the moon
Remained, the night's sole luminary. Then,
She too was blackened by this fearful cloud,
This formidable darkness, quite removed
From mortal gaze.

PHILEDEMON: That's nothing very strange.

PHILARETUS: Then lightning, thunder, screechings shook the heavens
And rent the sky. Chill horror numbed my sense
And froze my heart. Strange shapes there then appeared,
And faces that the shades themselves would dread.
Strange cries and roaring sounds were heard, and threats
That none could understand.

PHILEDEMON: Were you awake
Or sleeping when you saw this?

PHILARETUS: Why, awake
Most certainly.

PHILEDEMON: And then?

PHILARETUS: Then one, I thought,
Harangued them from on high, exclaiming loud:
'Let's hasten now'. Then like the lightning flash
All hurtled down to earth, and came to rest
Not far from here. While I, half dead with fright,
Sought house and home, resolved, at some fit hour,
To visit Cenodoxus and relate
The strange and wondrous visions I had seen.

PHILEDEMON: I'll come with you, and hear what Cenodoxus
Pronounces on this miracle of yours;
A man whose speech itself's a miracle,
New at each hearing. But where's Dama rushing?

PHILARETUS: Why are you panting so?

DAMA: Leave me.

PHILARETUS: Stop.

DAMA: No.
It's urgent.

PHILEDEMON: Is your master free?

DAMA: My master?

PHILEDEMON: Yes, master. We would like to visit him.

DAMA: Master! Don't ask!

PHILEDEMON: Boy, why prevaricate?

DAMA: Please let me go.

PHILEDEMON: No, not before you tell us.

DAMA: Pene perijt.   1185
PHILARETUS: Herus?
DAMA: Herus.
PHILARETUS: Tuus?
DAMA: Meus, inquio
    Cenodoxus: & penissime jam agit animam.
PHILEDEMON: Qui dum?
DAMA: Sub ingressum in aedes, concidit
    Recta, & repente viribus defectus est.
    Non caussa, non malo remedium extat palam.
    Aegre loquitur: arcessere medicos jubet;   1190
    Qui si morentur paululum, mox actum agent.
    Omitte plura. Propero.
PHILARETUS: Quid pertulit
    Cenodoxus infortunij?
PHILEDEMON: Quid uspiam
    Securitatis est? Quaeque gravia accidunt
    Mortalibus, se ut esse mortales sciant.   1195
    Frustra es, Philarete; adire, & audire haud licet
    Cenodoxon hodie.
PHILARETUS: Adibo nihilo ego sequius:
    Ut quem docentem audire non possum; queam
    Videre patientem. Dolorem vincere
    Certe docebit, ut aliud doceat nihil.   1200
    Exempla, quam lingua, efficacius docent.

SCENA VIII
PANURGUS, CHORUS MUSICUS CACODAEMONUM

    Nil aegrius mihi imperari a Numine
    Aliteque Numinis poterat, atque antea,
    Cum terrui, haud sane lubens, per somnia
    Cenodoxon. Heu, quid principi referam meo?   1205
    Ut me miseriter habebit, & crudeliter?
    Illine eosdem ego aucupor, & territos
    Rursus abigo, measque res idem augeo,
    Idemque perdo? forsitan minacijs
    Cenodoxus illis territus, mihi nuncium   1210
    Remittet? ad meum redire principem
    Nequeo, nisi Cenodoxus ad me redierit.

DAMA: He's almost dead.

PHILARETUS: The master?

DAMA: Yes.

PHILARETUS: Yours?

DAMA: Mine.
My master Cenodoxus, almost dead.

PHILEDEMON: What happened?

DAMA: Entering the house he fell
Headlong, and all his faculties have left him.
This illness manifests no cause or cure.
He hardly speaks. He's had the doctors summoned;
And if they waste a moment, they'll find him dead.
Enough now. I must fly.

PHILARETUS: What sad mischance
Has Cenodoxus suffered?

PHILEDEMON: Where, if anywhere,
Is anything secure? How sadly stricken
Are mortals, so they'll know their own mortality.
No use today; it would be too audacious
To be an audience to Cenodoxus.

PHILARETUS: I shall still go: if not to hear his teaching,
To see his patient suffering, for he'll show,
At least, how anguish can be overcome.
Thus may examples teach us more than words.

SCENE VIII
PANURGUS, CHOIR OF DEMONS

No worse command could Heaven and Heaven's angel
Force me unwillingly to obey: I've now
Terrified Cenodoxus in his dreams.
Alas, what shall I tell my prince of this?
How wretched will his cruelty render me!
Am I to stalk his almost-captured prey
Only to alarm and drive it off? Increase
My spoils and straightway lose them? Will these threats
Make Cenodoxus, terror-struck, renounce me?
If Cenodoxus won't return to me,
Neither can I return to face my prince.

Quid ordiar igitur ? arte jam contraria
Pugnabo. Terrere potui; potero etiam
Mulcere, palpo, voce, risu, musica.   1215
Nam & inferi testudine, cithara, chely
Novere ludere: neque tam fusci sumus,
Ut meticulosi somniant. Procurrite
Stygij choraulae: haec occupate limina
Fidium sonoro murmure, accinite, meras   1220
Beatitudines, suavitudines,
Ac dulcitudines meras: papavera,
Mulsa atque mella. Ego intus aegrum inducere
Molibor, ut se musica caelite putet
Recreari; Agite, & ostendite quid Orcus habeat   1225
Iucunditatis, si modo ea frui velit.

CHORUS

Desine coelum poscere questu,
Desine pectus tundere planctu,
Desine vultum perdere fletu;
Supera dudum Numen ab aula   1230
Faciles votis praestitit aures;
Nemo te adibit certius Astra.

PANURGUS: Reliquum ego pertexam. Ite, & Orcum, prodromi
Parate; certa est praeda nobis: commodum
Sequetur: ultimum instat illi praelium.   1235

What shall I do then? Use a different weapon.
I've shown the power to terrify, I'll show
The power to soothe, with laughter, song and music.
For devils too know how to play the lyre,
The lute and harp; we're not as black and raucous
As fearful people paint us in their dreams.
Come Stygian flutes, with heavenly murmurings
Make sonorous this threshold, sing delights
Of purest blessings, blandishments divine
And gentle joys: as sweet as poppy seed
With purest honey blended. I'll endeavour
To make the patient think he's being refreshed
By heavenly music. Show what sweet delights
Hell holds for him, if only he'll enjoy them.

CHOIR

> Cease from importuning heaven with complaining,
> Cease from your breast-beating and loud lamenting,
> Cease from disfiguring your face with your weeping;
> Long has the Lord from his high throne in heaven
> Heard all your praying with ears acquiescing;
> More than all others are you sure of glory.

PANURGUS: I'll do the rest. Go, harbingers, make sure
That Hell is ready; the prey is ours; he'll follow.
The final battle now draws nigh for him.

ACTUS IV

AESCULAPIUS: I Dama, nuncia venire, quos herus
  Vocaverat.
DAMA: Vocati adeste.
CENODOXUS: Accedite.
AESCULAPIUS: Dolemus aliquid accidisse tristius
  Cenodoxe; quod nostra tamen opera cito
  Curabitur; spondemus.   1240
CENODOXUS: Ille caelitum
  Quod Imperator jusserit, certum est sequi.
PHILAUTIA: Pie.
CENODOXUS: Mori perinde vivereque placet,
  Ut videro placere Numini.
MACHAON: Nihil
  Erit periculi.
PHILAUTIA: Pericula spernere
  Te finge.   1245
CENODOXUS: Nullum esse autumo periculum
  Quod ad beata me, & cupita littora
  Ejicit: ubi his carere tandem incommodis
  Malisque possiem.
PHILAUTIA: Quid his caelestius
  Pote dicier verbis?
PODALYRIUS: Carere nesciunt
  Haec saecula Cenodoxo: ut ille urbem hactenus   1250
  Servavit, ita decet hodie ut redhostiant.
AESCULAPIUS: Extende laevam, donec exploravero
  Venam. Machaon tange.

Act Four

SCENE I
AESCULAPIUS, MACHAON, PODALYRIUS,
DAMA, CENODOXUS, SELF-LOVE

AESCULAPIUS: Go, Dama, tell your master those he's summoned
    Have come.
DAMA: The men you summoned are here.
CENODOXUS: Approach.
AESCULAPIUS: We're grieved that some affliction, Cenodoxus,
    Has struck you down. But we can guarantee
    Our skill will cure you soon.
CENODOXUS: What God on high
    Is pleased to ordain, will surely come to pass.
SELF-LOVE: How pious.
CENODOXUS: To die, to live, both please me equally,
    If I can but please God.
MACHAON: You're surely not
    In any mortal danger.
SELF-LOVE: Affect contempt
    Of dangers.
CENODOXUS: I don't deem that dangerous
    Which bears me to those blessed shores, desired
    So long by me; where I can shed these cares
    And ills.
SELF-LOVE: What words more heavenly than these
    Can be expressed?
PODALYRIUS: This age is ill-equipped
    To lack a Cenodoxus; now must we
    Repay the care he's lavished on our city.
AESCULAPIUS: Stretch your left arm so I can see the artery.
    Touch him, Machaon.

MACHAON: Tremulus pulsus est,
Atque varius: modo nullus.
AESCULAPIUS: Etiam ut jacuerit
Vidistis? ut supinus? ut tetenderit   1255
Porrecta crura, manusque?
MACHAON: Non faustae nota
Est sanitatis.
PODALYRIUS: Ex notis ita dubijs
Atque subitis conjecto non dubium malum,
Celsusque mecum.
MACHAON: Assentior plenissime;
Eoque mage, quod brachia eadem cruraque   1260
Jactat frequentius.
AESCULAPIUS: Timentur haec quidem;
Sed longiori tantum in aegritudine.
Istaec dialis est. Licebit mitius
Pronuntiare.
PODALYRIUS: Non mihi.
MACHAON: Vitream date;
Valere non potest.   1265
AESCULAPIUS: Ut est livida? quasi
Tenuia quaedam fila subsidunt.
PODALYRIUS: Refert
Nubeculas quasi furfurum densissimas.
Vixit.
AESCULAPIUS: Ita me DEUS amet, haud temere anteidhac
Tam certa, tam subita indicia perspexeram
Mortis propinquae.   1270
MACHAON: Rursus accedere placet.
Caput aestuat.
PODALYRIUS: Cor tange.
CENODOXUS: Nemini alteri
Per me licebat pectus istud tangere;
Tu primus, idemque ultimus es.
MACHAON: Ingens calor
Praecordiorum, & cordis aestuatio.
Agitantur inibi venae, & impetu novo   1275
Feruntur.
AESCULAPIUS: Esse nihil periculosius
Queat. Quid agimus? de genere morbi haud liquet.
Medicina morbo incognito est incognita.
Placet opperiri crastinum.

MACHAON: His pulse is tremulous
    Intermittent; sometimes nil.
AESCULAPIUS: And do you see
    How limp he's lying? Legs and arms distended?
MACHAON: And these are hardly symptoms that suggest
    A healthy state.
PODALYRIUS: With dubious, sudden symptoms
    Like these, I diagnose along with Celsus
    A sure calamity.
MACHAON: My feelings quite;
    Especially seeing the frequent palsied shudders
    That shake his limbs.
AESCULAPIUS: Cause for concern, indeed;
    But only when a man's been ill for long.
    He's been ill just one day. We might pronounce
    A milder verdict.
PODALYRIUS: No.
MACHAON: Hand me the glass.
    He can't recover.
AESCULAPIUS: His urine's leaden coloured,
    With a deposit like fine threads.
PODALYRIUS: It's full
    Of black and murky spots, like some thick bran.
    He's done for.
AESCULAPIUS: Heavens! I've hardly ever seen
    Till now such sure and sudden signs that death
    Is imminent.
MACHAON: Let's have another look.
    His head's all hot.
PODALYRIUS: Now feel his heart.
CENODOXUS: I'll let
    No other person come and touch my chest.
    You're first, and last.
MACHAON: A heat immense and vast
    Inflames his diaphragm, his heart's on fire,
    His arteries all throbbing there, aglow
    With fresh attacks.
AESCULAPIUS: Than this there can be nothing
    More ominous. We cannot diagnose,
    Nor prescribe unknown cures for unknown ailments.
    We'll wait until tomorrow.

PODALYRIUS: Ipse crastinum
          Non opperibitur: morari non placet.   1280
MACHAON: Cenodoxe, ubi dolor tibi est acerrimus?
CENODOXUS: Perinde ubique. Pulmo tamen ardentius
          Prae caeteris divexat, & pleuritidis
          Stimuli coartant latera punctu perpete.
AESCULAPIUS: Praesentius nihil huic malo pellendo erit;   1285
          Pleuritidi quidem recenti Agallochum
          Potum ex aqua.
PODALYRIUS: Resinave terebynthina
          Lateri illita, aut apposita.
AESCULAPIUS: Sed pulmonibus
          Et herba Chrysocome bibita medebitur;
          Et Tragoriganon ex melle in eclegmate datum.   1290
PODALYRIUS & MACHAON: Ita convenit.
AESCULAPIUS: Duntaxat ut propere habeat.
CENODOXUS: I Dama, Pharmacopola ut istaec apparet
          Jube.
AESCULAPIUS: Bono animo es: reveniemus commodum
          Cenodoxe; & ut spero, meliuscule tuae
          Se res habebunt.   1295
CENODOXUS: Numini quod libuerit,
          Sperare libet.
PODALYRIUS: Animus mihi egregie dolet,
          Sperare me neque posse, neque promittere
          Tanto viro salutem.
MACHAON: Habet, quod perditus
          Orbis suam infelicitatem defleat,
          Qui tanta lumina nec diu, nec multa habet.   1300
AESCULAPIUS: Indignitas haec orbis est: nescit suam
          Opulentiam. Servare, colere oportuit
          Tales viros: quos negligit, coelum asserit.

SCENA II
HYPOCRISIS

          Extremus actus restat, Hypocrisis, tibi;
          Extrema pariter experiri convenit.   1305
          Cenodoxon educavi in hoc sinu meo:
          Simul senuimus. Quid aliud nunc est super,

PODALYRIUS: He'll not wait
    Until tomorrow. We've no time to waste.
MACHAON: Where do you feel the worst pain, Cenodoxus?
CENODOXUS: Equally everywhere. But principally my lungs
    Feel worse than all the rest, and pangs of pleurisy
    Contract my sides with constant stabs of pain.
AESCULAPIUS: We've nothing here to combat this infection.
    For incipient pleurisy we need some aloes
    Imbibed in water.
PODALYRIUS: Resin of turpentine
    Applied or rubbed into his side.
AESCULAPIUS: His lungs
    Can be relieved by herbal chrysocome;
    And goat's-thyme with an electuary of honey.
PODALYRIUS & MACHAON: We are agreed.
AESCULAPIUS: But he must have
    them soon.
CENODOXUS: Go Dama, give the chemist these prescriptions.
AESCULAPIUS: Keep up your spirits now, we'll come back soon,
    And hope to find you, Cenodoxus, feeling
    A little better.
CENODOXUS: We must match our hopes
    To God's designs.
PODALYRIUS: I'm very much distressed,
    For I can find no hope, promise no cure,
    For this great man.
MACHAON: His illness means the world,
    Bereft of him, must mourn its hapless loss,
    Where shining lights like him are few and brief.
AESCULAPIUS: This is the world's unworthiness; ignoring
    Its riches. Men like this it ought to cherish.
    When it neglects them, they are claimed by heaven.

SCENE II
HYPOCRISY

    The final act, Hypocrisy, is yours;
    And fitly this finality applied.
    I've brought up Cenodoxus as my own,
    We've aged together: what more likely now

Quam ne velit Cenodoxus absque me emori?
Hostes tamen vereor, & illos Caelites
Qui se suis adeo student clientibus   1310
Illosque sibi probare, saepe ut perditos
Orcique certos, ultima defenderint
Necessitate, & secum ad astra abduxerint.
Velut ego caeli saepe securissimos
Suprema in illa lucta ad Orcum compuli.   1315
Hic inter & Saxum, & Sacrum, pendent Stygis
Caelique spes: hic arma decretoria
Sumuntur: hic viribus opus validissimis
Arteque magistra; quam profiteor Hypocrisis.
Sed ne morando meque meaque negligam,   1320
Genium antevertam caelitem; neque patiar
Cenodoxum obaeratum mihi e manu rapi.

SCENA III
DAMA, CENODOXUS, HYPOCRISIS,
HUGO, PHILARETUS

DAMA: Here, nisi quod molestiae est, Hugo foris
     Philaretusque, aditum rogant.
CENODOXUS: Adducito.
HYPOCRISIS: Patientiam doloris hic ut jactites   1325
     Adverte: vim doloris aperi, dum tegis,
     Aut tegere velle crederis: itaque abditum
     Subinde compella dolorem: nihil agis
     Nil proficis vesane dolor; ut lancines
     Acerrime, superare non potes: tuas   1330
     Vincam ferendo insanias. Et id genus
     Alia. Modo adsunt; quod agis age.
CENODOXUS: O Philarete,
     O Hugo; satis an salve?
HUGO: Ego esse me rear
     Salvum absque Cenodoxo?
PHILARETUS: Mihi haud ita doleat
     Meus dolor, Cenodoxe, ut indolui tuo.   1335
CENODOXUS: Lectissimi juvenes, nimis amatis, scio,
     Cenodoxon. Imo injuriam prope facitis.
HUGO: Quid jam?

Than that he will refuse to die without me?
But yet I fear my foes, those heavenly beings,
Who guard their clients with such zealous care
And so commend themselves to them, defending,
Right to the last, souls lost and bound for Hell,
That they can save and lead them back to Heaven:
As I have often seized the safest souls,
Driven them Hellwards in that final battle.
Here on a razor's edge the hopes of Hell
And Heaven are poised; the crucial hosts are here
Arrayed; and all our strength is needed here,
And sovereign skill which I, Hypocrisy,
Profess. By no delay shall I neglect
My prey, or fail to anticipate the angel,
Or suffer Cenodoxus to be snatched from me.

SCENE III
DAMA, CENODOXUS, HYPOCRISY,
HUGO, PHILARETUS

DAMA: Philaretus and Hugo are outside,
      And wish to see you, if convenient.
CENODOXUS: Let them in.
HYPOCRISY: Take care to show how patiently
      You suffer pain: reveal its force while hiding it –
      Or seeming to be trying to hide it. Suddenly
      Address this hidden pain: 'Oh savage agony,
      You are achieving nothing; you may rage
      Most bitterly, but still you cannot conquer;
      I conquer by enduring your assaults!'
      And so on. Here they are. Go on.
CENODOXUS: My friends,
      Are you quite well?
HUGO: How can I think myself
      Well, without Cenodoxus?
PHILARETUS: All my pains
      Are nothing to the grief I've felt for you.
CENODOXUS: My dear young friends, I know your love is great –
      Too great; you almost harm your Cenodoxus.
HUGO: How?

CENODOXUS: Quia supra merita me mea colitis.
HYPOCRISIS: Recte, modeste.
HUGO: Novimus tua merita
    Cenodoxe, nostraque nomina: tuo non licet   1340
    Exire nobis aere. Sed quis lectulo
    Te casus afflixit?
CENODOXUS: Cave, Hugo, dixeris
    Casum: supremi jussa Numinis puta.
    Merentur id flagitia mea: quae mavelim
    Hic expiare, quibuslibet cruciatibus,   1345
    Quam Numine offenso hinc migrare.
HYPOCRISIS: Quam pie.
CENODOXUS: Sed unde nostis me non valere?
PHILARETUS: Civitas
    Prope universa dictitat, queritur, dolet.
CENODOXUS: Quae caussa luctus?
PHILARETUS: Tumet. Ille suo **Patri**,
    Alius Patrono, omnes amico clamitant   1350
    Malum accidisse grandius.
HYPOCRISIS: En, ut charus es!
    Quod tu doles, dolet omnibus.
CENODOXUS: Mihi vero nil
    Accidit, amici.
HUGO: Utinam quidem.
CENODOXUS: Sapientibus
    (Nec me tamen numeravero in sapientibus)
    Accidere quicquam posse credis? omnia   1355
    Paratus expectaveram, quae corpori
    Dudum minari caeperant. Ad hoc enim
    Ego memet auctoravi, & addixi libens,
    Perferre mortalia.
HYPOCRISIS: Nihil constantius.
CENODOXUS: Animus mihi hoc erectior, quo mage jacet   1360
    Corpus.
PHILARETUS: An ab istis mens doloribus nihil
    Turbatur?
CENODOXUS: A patientia ipse vincitur
    Dolor: nec ultra furere, quam in corpus sinit.
HUGO: Laudanda & admiranda prorsus haec tua est
    Constantia, Cenodoxe; nil doloribus   1365
    Concedere; affecto imperare corpori.

CENODOXUS: Since you praise me far beyond my due.

HYPOCRISY: How right and modest!

HUGO: We have known your merits
    And our own debt to you, a debt which never
    Can be repaid. But what sad chance confines you
    To bed?

CENODOXUS: Pray, Hugo, do not speak of it
    As chance; consider it Almighty God's
    Command. My sins deserve it. I'd prefer
    To expiate them here with torturing pains
    Than to depart with God's wrath unappeased.

HYPOCRISY: How pious.

CENODOXUS: Who told you I was ill?

PHILARETUS: The city
    Is full of talk and news and grief about it.

CENODOXUS: And why this grief?

PHILARETUS: Because of you. They all
    Lament that some great ill has struck you down,
    Their father, patron, friend.

HYPOCRISY: See how you're loved!
    Your grief grieves everyone.

CENODOXUS: Nothing disastrous
    Has happened to me, friends.

HUGO: Would that were true!

CENODOXUS: Do you believe that anything disastrous
    Can happen to the wise? (Not that I'll count
    Myself among them). Long have I been ready
    For every fleshly ill. I've pledged my life
    To this, and vowed to bear all mortal pains
    Most willingly.

HYPOCRISY: Who's seen such steadfastness!

CENODOXUS: My spirit soars the more affliction strikes
    My body down.

PHILARETUS: Is not the mind disturbed
    By such great pain?

CENODOXUS: By patience pain itself
    Is vanquished, on the flesh its force is spent.

HUGO: Your steadfastness must be admired and praised;
    Yielding no ground to pain and thus maintaining
    Such self-control, though in a frame so stricken.

Sed est molestum potius alijs, quam tibi,
Te aegrum esse.
CENODOXUS: Quomodo?
HUGO: Quia se dolent ope
Tua carere. Nos uterque principes
Ferimus moleste, aliique, quum te non licet   1370
Solito docentem attendere & obstupescere.
CENODOXUS: Lectissimi flores: docere jam quidem
Lingua nequit, occupata magno corporis
Incommodo: tolerantia atque robore
Animus docere potest. Facere non dicere   1375
Virtus docuit. Adeste, mecum temnite
Non aegritudinem modo, sed & ipsius
Adversa mortis tela. Nec modo spernite,
Verum appetite. Pulchrum est DEO spectaculum,
Hominem videre, cum doloribus & nece   1380
Compositum; eundem posse frangi, non tamen
Terrefieri, vincive. Mors mala non erit,
Nisi vita fuit. Et inanis est rei metus,
Augere quam timor potest, demere nequit.
Moriar? id expectaveram. Moriar? bene est;   1385
Ita desinam aegrotare posse; ita desinam
Posse alligari, posseque mori desinam.
Vivere juvat? Sed saepius taedet, piget.
Mori, semel fortasse piget; ubi vicero
Semel, pigere denuo haud potest. Brevis   1390
Vita fuit? imo longa nimium, si mala:
Si bona, satis longa fuit. Etenim sufficit
Breve spatium virtutibus: Paucos sibi
Annos requirunt: est satis vel unicus,
Satisque, nullus. Pluribus certe obfuit   1395
Vixisse, quam diem obisse.
PHILARETUS: Certe non eget
Solatio peregre petito, qui suo
Aeger valentes erigit.
HUGO: Multum doces
Cenodoxe, cum nihil etiam doces. Nequis
Vel aeger, alijs denegare utilem operam.   1400
CENODOXUS: O quanta pectori ingruit meo lues!
Ut asperat praecordia? ardent viscera!
Sed eiulare me dolor frustra jubes:
Nihil agis; imperabo.

Your illness is a worse distress to others
Than to yourself.

CENODOXUS: And why?

HUGO: Because they grieve
At being deprived of all your help. We two
And others grieve that no more, as we did,
Can we imbibe and marvel at your teaching.

CENODOXUS: Most favoured, blessed youths: my tongue can teach
No longer, overcome by fleshly ills.
But in endurance and in strength my spirit
Still can teach. To practise deeds, not words,
Virtue has taught me. Come, and with me scorn
Not only sickness but the very darts
Of death itself. And do not merely scorn death
But embrace it. How fair a sight for God
To see a man when faced with pain and death
Composed and calm; his body racked, his spirit
Unconquered, unafraid. His death's no evil
Unless his life was. How vain to fear a thing
Which fear can but increase and not diminish!
I'm dying? Good! What mortal does not die?
Death puts an end to sickness, and an end
To fleshly shackles – and an end to dying!
Is life a boon? It's often stale and loathsome.
Death may be loathsome once, but once achieved,
Has no more power to make me loathe again.
Was my life brief? No! far too long, if bad;
If good, then long enough. For virtues' flowering
A little span suffices; few the years
That they require. Just one may be enough,
Or less than one. Many have much more pain
In living than in dying.

PHILARETUS: He need seek
No comfort from another, when with his own
This sick man cheers the strong.

HUGO: How much you teach
Even when you're not teaching, Cenodoxus!
Though sick, you cannot cease from helping others.

CENODOXUS: What pestilence attacks my breast, what pain
Afflicts my heart! My entrails are on fire!
Anguish, you urge me uselessly to groan!
You achieve nothing! I'll prevail.

PHILARETUS: Lacrimas mihi
          Prope commovet, quum te video sine lacrimis   1405
          Tam gravia, tamque atrocia pati.
HYPOCRISIS: Bene premis
          Lamenta: ne patientiae laudem opprimas.
CENODOXUS: Aegre loquor. Revocate medicorum manum,
          Serpit malum: intercludit aegrum spiritum.
          Vis saeva me enicat. Aquulam huic incendio   1410
          Affundite. Aetnaeo camino calidior
          Populatur artus flamma. Sed nihil proficis
          Immane saevias licet: feram, feram.
HUGO: Obmutuit. Aquam adspergite: labra tingite.
PHILARETUS: Cenodoxe! nil movetur.   1415
HUGO: An animam forte agit?
PHILARETUS: Cenodoxe!
HUGO: Nictat, suspicit.
PHILARETUS: Qui vivimus
          Cenodoxe?
CENODOXUS: Vita in limine fuerat mea.
          Ite, medicos properate.
HUGO: Cedimus; DEUS
          Te sospitet, Cenodoxe.
CENODOXUS: Supremum vale
          Salveque Philarete; Hugo, mihi salve ac vale.   1420
HUGO: Nihil opus ita salvere, Cenodoxe: Superis
          Volentibus, salvum videre saepius
          Te licuerit.
PHILARETUS: Valente te valebimus.

SCENA IV
CHORUS ANGELORUM, lugentium,
CENODOXOPHYLAX

CHORUS: Quid se tuus habet alumnus? etiamnum tibi
          Resistit? an vicina mortis horula   1425
          Illum reduxit? quid taces?
CENODOXOPHYLAX: Socia cohors,
          Depositus est alumnus: illum jam salus
          Vix ipsa servet. Ita periculosus est
          Morbus animi, quem procreat superbia.

PHILARETUS: I'm moved
    Almost to tears on seeing you tearless suffer
    Such fearful anguish.
HYPOCRISY: See you suppress your moans,
    Lest they suppress their praise for your strong patience.
CENODOXUS: Call back the doctors. I can hardly speak.
    Disease invades me, quenching my faint spirit.
    Its fierce rage fells me. On this conflagration
    Pour water. Flames more fierce that Aetna's furnace
    Ravage my limbs. But you will not prevail,
    Rage though you may; I shall endure, endure.
HUGO: He's silent. Sprinkle water. Wet his lips.
PHILARETUS: Cenodoxus! He's quite still.
HUGO: Has he stopped breathing?
PHILARETUS: Cenodoxus!
HUGO: His eyelids flutter.
PHILARETUS: Cenodoxus,
    How are we now?
CENODOXUS: My life was on the brink.
    Go, make the doctors hurry.
HUGO: Yes, we're going.
    May God preserve you yet.
CENODOXUS: Take, Philaretus,
    My final salutation. Farewell, Hugo.
HUGO: Cenodoxus has no need of such farewells.
    God willing, we'll see you 'fare well' often yet.
PHILARETUS: When you are faring well then so shall we.

SCENE IV
CHORUS OF ANGELS, grieving,
CENODOXOPHYLAX

CHORUS: How is your ward? Does he resist you still?
    Or has the hour of his impending death
    Restored him to us? You're silent?
CENODOXOPHYLAX: Heavenly throngs,
    He's lost to us; even regaining health
    Could scarcely save him. So dangerous and dire
    The soul's disease that is the child of pride.

Virtute falsa contegit verum scelus: 1430
Nescitque vulnus, vulneratus undique,
Aut spernit atque negligit, quoad interit.
Reperere nempe scelera ad excidium hominis
Compendiariam hanc viam, ut virtutibus
Velata, nescirentur, hominemque inscium   1435
Prope, & nihil timentem ad Orci limina
Deponerent.

CHORUS: Oportet pertinaciter
Monere, nihil omittere, omnia dicere,
Omniaque facere: fortean tandem dabit
Manus.   1440

CENODOXOPHYLAX: Monemus imo, & aures vellimus
Animosque nostris saepe alumnis: nil tamen
Proficimus: adeo se suos non autumant,
Ut viliores sint sibi ipsis, quam suis
Sint hostibus.   1444

CHORUS
Fundite fletus, tundite pectus,   1445
Edite planctus, promite luctus;
Sidera vilis spernit homullus,
Tartara charus quaerit alumnus.

CENODOXOPHYLAX: Jam machinationibus   1444
Cenodoxus oppugnatur acriter omnibus;
At ipse denudatus est; undique patet   1450
Locus hosti; amicum credit.   1451

CHORUS
Quid casso, socij, labore vilem
Dignamur toties adire terram?
Ipsi cedere nos jubent amici,
Ipsi pellere nos solent alumni.   1455

CENODOXOPHYLAX: Ibo, & opem feram.   1451
Heu monstra stygia; heu inferas acies! mihi
Vix aditus est.

He covers real transgression with false virtue,
Ignorant of wounds, though wounded everywhere,
He scorns and disregards them, till he dies.
For sins have found a way to ruin man
Easy and quick, veiling themselves in virtues,
So that, unrecognised, they lead him fearless,
Almost unknowing, till they set him down
By the very gates of Hell.

CHORUS: He must be warned
Persistently, unsparingly; no deed
Or word untried; perhaps he'll yet deliver
Himself to us.

CENODOXOPHYLAX: We do exhort our wards,
Battering their ears and hearts continually,
In vain. So little do they rate their worth,
They make themselves more worthless to themselves
Than to their enemies.

CHORUS

Pour out your tears now, beat on your breast now,
Show forth your grieving, send forth your wailing;
Frail earthly man despises the heavens,
Hell is the choice of the dear ones we've cherished.

CENODOXOPHYLAX: Fiercely beset
By every treacherous wile is Cenodoxus.
But he's defenceless, open to all attacks
From the foe he thinks his friend.

CHORUS

Why with vain toil do we honour so often
This vile worthless world with our heavenly presence?
Even our friends give us orders to leave them,
Even our wards themselves drive us away.

CENODOXOPHYLAX: I'll go and help.
Ah! spectres, hosts of hell! They almost block
My way to him.

SCENA V

CENODOXOPHYLAX, PANURGUS,
HYPOCRISIS, PHILAUTIA

CENODOXOPHYLAX: Quid juris in alumnum meum
    Vobis, scelesti, sumitis?
PANURGUS: Quid in meum
    Tibi juris est?
CENODOXOPHYLAX: Tuumne dicis?
PANURGUS: Inquio.
CENODOXOPHYLAX: Qua fronte? monstrum.   1460
PANURGUS: Qua soleo.
CENODOXOPHYLAX: Plagiarius
    Nefandus es.
PANURGUS: Sese mihi in meam fidem
    Ultro ipse dedit.
CENODOXOPHYLAX: Ecquae fides enim tua?
    Perfide.
PANURGUS: Vel hinc quae sit, scies; nunquam feram
    Ut hunc, alumnum vel tuum tu appellites,
    Meum vel esse neges.   1465
CENODOXOPHYLAX: Datus a DEO est mihi.
PANURGUS: At scelera fecerunt meum.
CENODOXOPHYLAX: Fieri meus.
    Jam denuo potest.
PANURGUS: Meusque denuo
    Potest.
CENODOXOPHYLAX: Apage te.
PANURGUS: Apage te.
CENODOXOPHYLAX: Adhuc resipiscere
    Moram habet.
PANURGUS: Adhuc plus desipiscere moram habet.
CENODOXOPHYLAX: Quid si reduxero?   1470
PANURGUS: Quid si ego iterum abduxero?
CENODOXOPHYLAX: Non hinc recedes?
PANURGUS: Imo, cum recesserit
    Cenodoxus.
CENODOXOPHYLAX: Eheu; misera sors miseri hominis!
    Et quid sorores inde geminae Tartari?
    Quid quaeritatis?
HYPOCRISIS: Nostrum herum, cui sedulo
    Servivimus.   1475

SCENE V
CENODOXOPHYLAX, PANURGUS,
HYPOCRISY, SELF-LOVE

CENODOXOPHYLAX: What right have you to approach
    My ward, you fiends of hell?
PANURGUS: What right have *you*
    To approach *my* ward?
CENODOXOPHYLAX: You call him yours?
PANURGUS: I do.
CENODOXOPHYLAX: With such effrontery?
PANURGUS: Such is my custom.
CENODOXOPHYLAX: Vile trafficker in souls!
PANURGUS: Quite voluntarily
    He came into my trust.
CENODOXOPHYLAX: What trust or faith
    Have you, perfidious rogue?
PANURGUS: You'll know from this:
    I'll never let you call this man your ward,
    Or say that he's not mine.
CENODOXOPHYLAX: God gave him to me.
PANURGUS: His sins have made him mine.
CENODOXOPHYLAX: He can again
    Be mine.
PANURGUS: And once again he can be mine.
CENODOXOPHYLAX: Be off.
PANURGUS: Be off!
CENODOXOPHYLAX: He still has time to regain
    His senses.
PANURGUS: And time to lose them all the more.
CENODOXOPHYLAX: What if I lead him back?
PANURGUS: What if I lead him
    Astray again?
CENODOXOPHYLAX: Won't you be gone?
PANURGUS: I'll go,
    When Cenodoxus goes.
CENODOXOPHYLAX: Ah! wretched man's
    Most wretched fate! And Hell's twin sisters, what
    Do you seek here?
HYPOCRISY: Our master whom so zealously
    We've served.

PHILAUTIA: Nostrum imo mancipium, cui
    Diu imperavimus.
PANURGUS: Tibi nec servijt,
    Nec tu imperasti.
CENODOXOPHYLAX: Eheu, nimis quam scio probe.
PANURGUS: Proinde jus hic quaere nullum.
HYPOCRISIS: Nullus es;
    Obsurduit tibi Cenodoxus: mihi vigil
    Utramque praebet aurem.   1480
PHILAUTIA: Ego animum retineo
    Arctis ligatum vinculis.
CENODOXOPHYLAX: O quam graves,
    Cenodoxe, dominos pateris?
HYPOCRISIS: Atque quam gravem,
    Cenodoxe, dominum fugis, ubi hunc fugis. Equidem
    Tibi gloriamque dignitatemque peperi.
    Hic perdere cupit.   1485
CENODOXOPHYLAX: Parere volui, haud perdere,
    Sed veriorem: haec vana, fluxa, nulla erit.
PHILAUTIA: Ego unice studui, ut placeres omnibus,
    Hic displicere omnibus, omnia tibique vult.
CENODOXOPHYLAX: Imo placeres ut DEO, hoc contenderam.
    Jam nec placere DEO, nec homini tu potes.   1490
PANURGUS: Imo potes & DEO & homini. Nihil ambige.
    Perspecta virtus enitet.
CENODOXOPHYLAX: Quaenam enitet
    Virtus?
HYPOCRISIS: Misericordia tua adversus inopes,
    Studium benevolentiaque in omnes: Sanctitas
    Viventis, & pietas precantis. Caeteram   1495
    Quid memoro virtutem polo dignam, & DEO?
CENODOXOPHYLAX: Benefacere, Cenodoxe, nil juvat; nisi
    Demissa mens accesserit.
HYPOCRISIS: Laudem licet
    Virtuti habere.
CENODOXOPHYLAX: Ambire vero, non licet.
PHILAUTIA: Virtus videri debet.   1500
CENODOXOPHYLAX: Ipsa non cupit.
PHILAUTIA: Quaerenda gloria erat.
CENODOXOPHYLAX: Erat; sed verior;
    Haec vana, cassa, falsa, fluxa, nulla erat.

SELF-LOVE: We seek our slave, you mean, the man
    Who's long obeyed our orders.

PANURGUS: He's not *your* slave
    Nor you his master.

CENODOXOPHYLAX: I know all too well
    That's true.

PANURGUS: So seek no jurisdiction here.

HYPOCRISY: You've lost; for Cenodoxus will not hear you.
    His ears are mine alone.

SELF-LOVE: I hold his heart
    Bound fast to me with chains.

CENODOXOPHYLAX: Oh, Cenodoxus,
    You tolerate harsh masters!

HYPOCRISY: Harsh the master
    You flee from, Cenodoxus, fleeing him.
    I've brought you glory and great honours, he
    Wants you to lose them.

CENODOXOPHYLAX: No, to bring, not lose
    A truer glory; this one's vain, frail, fleeting.

SELF-LOVE: I've striven to make you please all men. His aim
    Is that you should please none, and nothing please you.

CENODOXOPHYLAX: My aim indeed was that you should please God.
    But now you can please neither God nor man.

PANURGUS: You can please God, and man. Do not doubt this.
    Your beacon virtue shines.

CENODOXOPHYLAX: What shining virtue
    May this be?

HYPOCRISY: Your compassion for the poor,
    Your fond concern and care for all, your sanctity
    Of life, your pious prayers. And not to mention
    More virtues worthy of high heaven and God!

CENODOXOPHYLAX: Good works will profit nothing, Cenodoxus,
    Without humility.

HYPOCRISY: Praise should be given
    For such great virtue.

CENODOXOPHYLAX: It should not be sought.

SELF-LOVE: But virtue should be seen.

CENODOXOPHYLAX: This virtue shuns.

SELF-LOVE: And glory must be sought.

CENODOXOPHYLAX: Yes, truer glory.
    This glory's false and fleeting, idle, vain.

PHILAUTIA: Haec magna, vera, clara, pulchra, aeterna erat.

CENODOXOPHYLAX: Peritura jam jam.

PHILAUTIA: Vivere imo clarius
    Jam denique incaeptura.   1505

CENODOXOPHYLAX: Sidera aspice
    Cenodoxe; quid tibi potest praeclarius
    Illa videri gloria ? hanc petas licet.

HYPOCRISIS: Terras videto; tanta tamque patentia
    Orbis spatia; quid rarius, quid charius,
    Quid clarius, quam posse fama & nomine   1510
    Tuo replere haec cuncta ? Nosci ab omnibus ?
    Coli, atque amari ? postque cineres vivere ?
    Superesse posteris ? nec ullis saeculis
    Senescere !

CENODOXOPHYLAX: Quid inde lucrifeceris ? petens
    Famam deperdita anima ? Si orbem gloria   1515
    Habebit, animam Tartara. Huc te advertito
    Cenodoxe.

PANURGUS: Te huc advertito.

CENODOXOPHYLAX: Hunc tu ne audias
    Cenodoxe.

PANURGUS: Tu ne hunc audias.

CENODOXOPHYLAX: Inimicus est.

PANURGUS: Inimicus est: fallere cupit.

CENODOXOPHYLAX: Perdere cupit;
    Ego te adjuvare.   1520

PANURGUS: Ego te adjuvare.

HYPOCRISIS: Recte agis
    Cenodoxe; Jam sapis.

CENODOXOPHYLAX: Male agis, ac desipis.

PHILAUTIA: In orbe jam laudaberis.

CENODOXOPHYLAX: In Orco, miser,
    Damnaberis.

PHILAUTIA: Dicere sanctus.

CENODOXOPHYLAX: Improbus
    Dicere.

PANURGUS: Saeculique decus.

CENODOXOPHYLAX: Ah dedecus.

PHILAUTIA: Virtutis exemplum.   1525

CENODOXOPHYLAX: Sceleris.

HYPOCRISIS: Omnes scient
    Laudes tuas.

SELF-LOVE: This glory's great and true, fair and eternal.

CENODOXOPHYLAX: It's doomed to perish now.

SELF-LOVE: To live more gloriously
   From now.

CENODOXOPHYLAX: Gaze, Cenodoxus, at the stars.
   What can you see more noble than the radiance
   Of their great glory? This glory you should seek.

HYPOCRISY: Behold the earth, the great and far-flung lands
   Of this terrestrial globe. What rarer, fairer,
   More glorious than to make all these resound
   With your great name and fame? Be known by all?
   Be loved and cherished? And, when your body's dust,
   To live for all posterity, never withering
   From age to age?

CENODOXOPHYLAX: What will you gain by this?
   Seeking for glory at your soul's perdition?
   Your fame may hold the world: Hell holds your soul.
   Gaze here.

PANURGUS: Gaze here.

CENODOXOPHYLAX: Don't listen, Cenodoxus.

PANURGUS: Don't listen to him.

CENODOXOPHYLAX: He's your enemy.

PANURGUS: He's your sworn foe. He's trying to deceive you.

CENODOXOPHYLAX: He seeks to damn and I to help you.

PANURGUS: I
   Am helping.

HYPOCRISY: Sound, wise Cenodoxus!

CENODOXOPHYLAX: Foolish!

SELF-LOVE: The world will sing your praises.

CENODOXOPHYLAX: And in Hell
   You will be damned.

SELF-LOVE: Be called a saint.

CENODOXOPHYLAX: A sinner.

PANURGUS: The glory of the age.

CENODOXOPHYLAX: A burning shame.

SELF-LOVE: Virtue's epitome.

CENODOXOPHYLAX: No, sin's.

HYPOCRISY: All men
   Shall know your fame.

CENODOXOPHYLAX: Fraudes tuas.
HYPOCRISIS: Te ora omnium
    Ferent.
CENODOXOPHYLAX: Prement.
HYPOCRISIS: Amabit orbis.
CENODOXOPHYLAX: Oderit.
HYPOCRISIS: Te praedicabit.
CENODOXOPHYLAX: Elevabit te.
HYPOCRISIS: Colet.
CENODOXOPHYLAX: Tollet. Adeone despicatui te habes,
    Cenodoxe, ut hostibus tuis, plus quam tuo   1530
    Fidas patrono?
PANURGUS: Haud est patronus.
PHILAUTIA: Et tui
    Quid inquient, quid audient clientium
    Greges, nisi tuam gloriam extremum tenes?
CENODOXOPHYLAX: Quid inquiet caeleste Numen? caelites
    Quid inquient, nisi gloriam tandem hanc fugis?   1535
PANURGUS: Ingratus & molestus, ac dudum gravis
    Apud meum es Cenodoxum. Abi, & meam mihi
    Relinque praedam.
CENODOXOPHYLAX: Immeritus odio sum. Fugit
    Sana Cenodoxus, improba modo quaeritat
    Consilia. Lusus inferis cohortibus   1540
    Abeo. Tonantem flectere precibus meis
    Fortasse quibo. Non mihi parcam, ut meo
    (Heu non meo) velit ille alumno parcere.

SCENA VI
DAMA, AESCULAPIUS,
MACHAON, PODALYRIUS

DAMA: Seri estis: eluctatur animus egredi
    E corpore.   1545
AESCULAPIUS: Meliora superi.
DAMA: Accurrite.
MACHAON: Cenodoxe. Surdo.
PODALYRIUS: Deficitur aeger animo
    Totus.
AESCULAPIUS: Date huc buglosson, ori ut ingeram.

CENODOXOPHYLAX: Your shame.
HYPOCRISY: Your name will be
    On all men's lips.
CENODOXOPHYLAX: On none.
HYPOCRISY: The world will love you.
CENODOXOPHYLAX: Hate–
HYPOCRISY: Extol–
CENODOXOPHYLAX: Disdain–
HYPOCRISY: Cherish–
CENODOXOPHYLAX: Erase you.
    Why, do you hold yourself in such contempt,
    That, Cenodoxus, you've more faith in foes
    Than in your guardian?
PANURGUS: No guardian he!
SELF-LOVE: And then
    What will your host of clients say and think
    Unless you keep your glory to the end?
CENODOXOPHYLAX: What will God say, and all the heavenly host,
    Unless you shun this glory at the end?
PANURGUS: You are unwelcome, tiresome, burdensome
    Over my Cenodoxus. Go, leave my prey
    To me.
CENODOXOPHYLAX: All undeserving am I hated.
    Good advice Cenodoxus shuns, and bad
    He hankers for. Mocked by the hosts of hell
    I go. Perhaps my prayers may still appease
    God's majesty. I'll spare no pains, that God
    May spare my ward, alas, my ward no longer.

SCENE VI
DAMA, AESCULAPIUS,
MACHAON, PODALYRIUS

DAMA: You are too late. His soul strives from his body
    To be released.
AESCULAPIUS: May heaven forbid!
DAMA: Come quickly.
MACHAON: Cenodoxus! No response.
PODALYRIUS: He's quite inert.
AESCULAPIUS: Give me some ox-tongue, and I'll feed him.

PODALYRIUS: Habes.

AESCULAPIUS: Revomit.

PODALYRIUS: At denuo ingere.

AESCULAPIUS: Reijcit.

MACHAON: Pulejum aceto fractum ad imas admove
     Nares.   1550

AESCULAPIUS: Nihil ago. Nulla virtus. Respuit
     Medicamina malum.

PODALYRIUS: Jam pedes extendere
     Occoepit. Omnis calor abit: frigidus habet
     Extrema sudor membra. Proximum est mori.

MACHAON: Adeo repentinum malum, pestem, necem
     Nunquam videre memini.   1555

PODALYRIUS: An expiaverat
     Animum prius, quam hic ageret animam?

DAMA: Maximo
     Cum sensu: & ipse lacrimis madidas genas
     Manare vidi.

MACHAON: Pastus epulo etiam est sacro?

DAMA: Sanctissime: movitque fletum astantibus
     Flens ipse. Verba semifracta, sed novam   1560
     Prae se ferentia sanctitatem identidem
     Iterans: nec ante sancta desijt loqui,
     Quam desierat omnino proloqui.

AESCULAPIUS: Decet,
     Moriatur ut sancte ille, qui sic vixerat.
     Sed adeste; concedamus hinc; nihil opera   1565
     Jam nostra mortuum juvat. Nam mortuum
     Vocitare Cenodoxum dolore maximo
     Cogor.

SCENA VII

PANURGUS, PHILAUTIA, CHORUS CACODAEMONUM, insultantium,
MORS (HYPOCRISIS, SPIRITUS CENODOXI,
CENODOXOPHYLAX)

PANURGUS: Modo apparatus est stygia locus
     Palude: quid moraris emori? Nequis
     Vitam precario redimere. Nequis meas   1570
     Evadere manus.

PODALYRIUS: Here.

AESCULAPIUS: He vomits it up.

PODALYRIUS: Then try once more.

AESCULAPIUS: No good.

MACHAON: Let us apply some fleabane mixed with vinegar,
    Under his nostrils.

AESCULAPIUS: No. No use. His malady
    Rejects all medicine.

PODALYRIUS: With sudden stiffening
    His legs are paralysed. All warmth has gone.
    His limbs are cold with sweat. He's near to death.

MACHAON: Such sudden sickness, fatal, dire contagion
    I can't remember seeing.

PODALYRIUS: Did he confess
    His sins before he died?

DAMA: Most movingly.
    I saw the tears come welling in his eyes.

MACHAON: Did he receive communion?

DAMA: Most piously.
    And moved to tears those standing by his bed,
    In tears himself. His barely uttered words
    Proclaimed a sanctity of a new kind,
    Not seen before. And holy words ceased only
    When all speech failed him, not till then.

AESCULAPIUS: How fitting.
    His life deserves a holy, saintly death.
    But come, let us depart, we can do nothing
    To help the dead; for, with the greatest sorrow,
    I am compelled to say that Cenodoxus
    Is dead.

SCENE VII

PANURGUS, SELF-LOVE, CHORUS OF DEVILS, mocking
Cenodoxus, DEATH (HYPOCRISY, CENODOXUS' SPIRIT,
CENODOXOPHYLAX)

PANURGUS: Your place in Hell's foul swamps is ready.
    Why do you take so long to die? No prayers
    Can buy you back your life. You can't escape
    My claws.

PHILAUTIA: Evome animam. Tartaro
Hanc hostiam debes, mihique hoc praemium.

PANURGUS: Istaec manus te expectat; hos ungues tibi
Defigere aveo.

ASEMPHOLOTH: Jam profugere non potes
Cavea mea.   1575

PHASALLIOTH: Revertere ad Numen nequis:
Jam non receptat, saepius vocaverat,
Sed abnuisti. Quid moraris emori!

HYPOCRISIS: Frustra ingemiscis. Cingere, morere, sequere
Cocyti ad antra, sceleribus meritas tuis
Sedes; superbus ad superbos; improbus   1580
Ad improbos.   1581

CHORUS CACODAEMONUM
Triumphate, cachinnate, reserate Tartara,
Jam superba anhelamus, & raptamus spolia.
Asempholoth, Phasallioth, & Asteroth hiascite,
Faucibus & rictibus hanc belluam immergite.   1585
Jam propinquat mors tremenda, mors horrenda jaculo:
Jam fas erit harpagare, deturbare Tartaro.

MORS: Regina terrae, quae mea   1581
Framea feroces frango Regum spiritus.
Quicquid potens est, arbores, saxa, oppida,
Ferrumque chalybemque domo. Quicquid in aere,   1590
Quicquid profundo, quicquid ista gignitur
Tellure; fasces undique horret ad meos.
Nec tu, nec iste, nec ille, nec quisquis alius
Hoc spiculum non sentiet. Saepe pueros,
Saepe Juvenes, semper senes mihi subigo,   1595
Hoc clepsydrae reliquum quod est, conceditur
Parisiaco Doctori; ut audio, inclyto
Viro; sed inclytus licet sit, non movet;
Morietur; appetit mora extremissima.
Compono telum; libro, vibro, figo.   1600

OMNES: Habet;
Vicimus.

SPIRITUS: Heu, heu.

PANURGUS: Ad inferos; ad inferos.

CENODOXOPHYLAX: Mane
Panurge.

SELF-LOVE: Spew out your soul. To Hell you owe
    This victim, and to me this recompense.

PANURGUS: These hands await you and these nails are craving
    To fasten into you.

ASEMPHOLOTH: You can't escape
    My clutches now.

PHASALLIOTH: You can't return to God:
    He won't receive you now. He often called you,
    But you rejected Him. Why don't you die?

HYPOCRISY: Your groans are unavailing. Rise and follow
    Into the depths of Hell, a region suitable
    For sins like yours: proud to the proud, and impious
    To the impious.

CHORUS OF DEVILS
    Sound the triumph, raise the laughter, open up the gates of Hell,
    Now we close on, chase and pounce on, snatch and seize the
      spoils so proud.
    Asempholoth, Phasallioth, and Asteroth, bare your fangs,
    Open up your gaping jaws and grab, devour this
      monstrous prey
    Fearful death is fast approaching, poised to hurl his fatal dart;
    Then our prey is ours, to claw him, bear him down with us
      to Hell.

DEATH: Ruler of earth, I pierce
    The hearts of earth's proud rulers with my dart.
    I tame the power of all: trees, rocks, proud towns,
    Iron, steel. Whatever in the air or sea
    Or on the land itself comes into being
    Is fearful of my might on every side.
    Not you, nor he, nor any will escape
    This sting of mine. For often I subdue
    Young children; often youths; old men invariably.
    This glass contains the few last grains of life
    Left to a Paris doctor–famed, I hear!
    However great his fame, it will not move me;
    He dies! His very final moment's come.
    I poise and aim my dart and drive it home.

ALL: He's dead. We've won.

SPIRIT: Ah, ah.

PANURGUS: To Hell, to Hell.

CENODOXOPHYLAX: Panurgus, wait.

PANURGUS: Non maneo.
CENODOXOPHYLAX: Impero.
PANURGUS: Quid jam rei?
CENODOXOPHYLAX: Supplicia differ. Judicem prius audiat
    Cenodoxus! illic interim asserva reum.
MORS: In uno nequeo conquiescere.   1605
    Plures adeo. Regumque turres, pauperum
    Velut tabernas pulso, verto, subruo.
    Nunc quaerito, quis proximus sit debitor.

SCENA VIII
CHORUS MORTUALIS

    Sic transit mundi gloria
      Cum sequuntur funera.   1610
    Omnis enim dignitas
      Mera est inanitas.
    Heri plenus honoribus,
      Cras erit esca vermibus.
    Cras infestabit vipera,   1615
      Quem nunc honestat purpura.
  Beati rector Seculi,
  Parce terrae pulveri.
    Nulla cavet prudentia
      Mortis stratagemata.   1620
    Nulla flectit potentia,
      Iratae mortis brachia.
    Nulla fallit solertia,
      Astutae mortis spicula.
  O Magni virtus Numinis,   1625
  Quid est vita hominis?
    Vixdum bene nascimur
      Cum repente morimur:
    Vita enim hominum,
      Nil est nisi somnium.   1630

PANURGUS: No.
CENODOXOPHYLAX: I command you.
PANURGUS: Why?
CENODOXOPHYLAX: Postpone the punishment. Let Cenodoxus
    First hear the judgement. Meanwhile, guard him there.
DEATH: I cannot rest with one. I must find more.
    Kings' palaces, the hovels of the poor,
    I knock at all alike, and rout them all.
    Now I must find the next whose debt is due.

SCENE VIII
FUNERAL CHORUS

> Thus terrestrial glory fades
> When the funeral pomp is done;
> Every human dignity
> Is merely vain inanity.
> Yesterday's great man of honours,
> Food for worms he'll be tomorrow;
> Vipers will infest tomorrow
> The man who's robed in state to-day.
>   Ruler of those blest forever
>   Spare the dust of mortal clay.
> No kind of prudence whatsoever
> Guards against the wiles of death.
> No power, however strong, can sever
> The strangle-hold of angry death.
> Guile and skill can ne'er deflect
> The stings and darts of artful death.
>   Oh Power that can all heaven scan,
>   What is the life of mortal man?
> Scarcely are we born at all
> Than we death's sudden victims fall;
> So must this life of mortals seem
> Nothing but an empty dream.

ACTUS V

SCENA I
CHRISTUS, D. PETRUS, D. PAULUS,
Cum alijs judicibus,
D. MICHAEL, CENODOXOPHYLAX, SPIRITUS CENODOXI,
CONSCIENTIA, PANURGUS

CHRISTUS: Arcessite Cenodoxum; & absque mora meum
    Hoc ad tribunal sistite. Actio dabitur.
MICHAEL: Cenodoxe adesdum ad Judicem: in jus ambula.
SPIRITUS: Etiam sequere tu! vocata non eras.
CONSCIENTIA: Venio invocata. Sequar: loquar, quicquid sciam.   1635
SPIRITUS: Abscede: solus ibo.
CONSCIENTIA: Nunquam avellar hinc;
    Aeterna comes haerebo Conscientia.
MICHAEL: Ut jusseras, incoram adest, aequissime
    Judex.
CHRISTUS: Et accusator ut veniat, jube.
MICHAEL: Panurge mox praesto sis, dabitur actio: 1640
    Comparet.
CHRISTUS: Hunc tu noscis?
PANURGUS: Ut nemo melius.
CHRISTUS: Tu facta, dicta, cogitata singula
    Es arbitratus?
PANURGUS: Omnia sagacissime.
CHRISTUS: Tuque Cenodoxophylax?
CENODOXOPHYLAX: In acta sedulo
    Cuncta retuli.   1645
CHRISTUS: Quare agite lege: jus dabo.
SPIRITUS: O parce Judex, parce tam severiter
    Exigere caussas; Nequeo vincere, nequeo
    Hac lege. Misericordiam supplex rogo.

Act Five

CHRIST, ST PETER, ST PAUL,
With the other judges,
ST MICHAEL, CENODOXOPHYLAX, SPIRIT OF
CENODOXUS, CONSCIENCE, PANURGUS

CHRIST: Bid Cenodoxus come, appear straightway
    Before this court. His case will now be heard.
MICHAEL: Cenodoxus, come to court and face the judge.
SPIRIT: Do you come too? You were not bidden here.
CONSCIENCE: I come unbidden, to testify all I know.
SPIRIT: Depart; I'll go alone.
CONSCIENCE: I'll never leave you.
    I'll cling to you, your everlasting shadow.
MICHAEL: As you commanded, here is the accused,
    Most just of judges.
CHRIST: Bid his accuser come.
MICHAEL: Panurgus come, the court's in session. He's here.
CHRIST: Do you know the accused?
PANURGUS: Better than anyone.
CHRIST: And have you weighed each single deed and word
    And thought of his?
PANURGUS: Most keenly, every one.
CHRIST: And you, his guardian angel?
CENODOXOPHYLAX: I have most faithfully
    Recorded everything.
CHRIST: Proceed. I shall give judgement.
SPIRIT: Forbear, oh judge, with such severity
    To examine this case. If such strict law's enforced,
    I cannot win. My humble plea is 'mercy'.

CHRISTUS: Nihil audio. Tu siqua dicere habes; licet.

PANURGUS: Severe, Magne, juste Judex: dicere   1650
     Ea me jubes, quae, me tacente, noveras
     Et improbaras ipse pridem: dicere
     Tamen aggrediar, eoque dicam audentius,
     Quod causa non tam agenda, quam acta videbitur.
     Nec enim meis graviora dictis fecero   1655
     Hujus facinora; qui studuit ita improbus
     Ita semper esse perditus, nihil ut mihi
     Reliquerit, quod adderem aut affingerem.
     Nam alios subinde singula vitia singulos
     Traxere; verum hunc omnia: Omnia, inquio   1660
     Audaciter; non fallo. Taceam singula,
     Verbo omnia uno dixero: Superbus est.
     Vici; Superbus est. Nec aliud affero,
     Jam dicta caussa est. Scelera ibi omnia collocant
     Sedem, ubi Superbia. Te tuumque aequissimum   1665
     Testor tribunal; Expulit nos unicum
     Hoc crimen, aula caelitum; idque solvimus
     Non unicum; fuere enim inibi plurima
     Scelera, ubi sola repperta est Superbia.
     Ergone caelo ejeceris, quos videras   1670
     Superbientes; hunc tumentem gloria
     Receperis? Caelo asseratur ille, qui
     Semper mea imperata, qui nunquam tua
     Fecit? Beata cui fuit ludibrio
     Curia, beatus audiat? qui nomine   1675
     Ductuque & auspicio omnia egerit meo,
     Stipendia prope innumera sub me fecerit,
     Adversus auctorem suum pugnaverit,
     Seclusus a me vivat? aut tua aequitas
     Judex, labascit; aut mihi hunc addicito.   1680

SPIRITUS: Miserere Judex; parcite reo Judices.

PANURGUS: Nondum peroravi. Vide quis hunc stupor
     Vexarit! a te conditum se meminerat,
     (Sed mentior; non meminerat; nam gratior
     Foret, memor si esset.) tamen se conditum   1685
     A te sciebat, atque multis praemijs
     Identidem ad beatiora praemia
     Vocari; at abnuit, refugit, restitit.
     Me vix vocantem, pollicentem inania

CHRIST: I will not hear you. Let the accuser speak.

PANURGUS: Most just and mighty judge, you bid me speak
     Of things that you have known without my telling
     And long condemned. Yet I will speak of them,
     And speak the more audaciously because
     My case, being proved already, scarce needs proof.
     Nor shall I aggravate with words of mine
     The burden of his sins, for his corruption
     Was so incorrigible and deliberate,
     There is no scope to adorn or add to it.
     One single vice has ruined other men.
     This man has every vice–yes, all, I say,
     And dare say, for I'm right. Omitting detail,
     They're comprehended in one word: he's proud.
     I've won: he's proud. No other count I bring,
     My case rests here. For where pride has its seat,
     All other sins are found. Most just of judges,
     To you I make appeal: this single sin
     Drove us from heaven. We paid for others too;
     For many other sins were there involved,
     Though pride alone discovered. And shall you,
     Who hurled us out of heaven because you saw
     That we were proud, take this pride-bloated mortal
     Into your keeping? Shall he be claimed by heaven,
     Who always did *my* bidding, never *yours*?
     Shall he, who parodied heaven's hosts of blessed,
     Hear them in blessedness? Whose every deed
     Was done at my behest and in my name,
     Who served for countless years under my flag,
     Fighting his own creator, shall this man
     Be sundered from me? Judge, your very justice
     Is fallible, unless you judge him mine.

SPIRIT: Oh judge, have mercy; judges, spare the accused.

PANURGUS: I've not yet done. See with what idiocy
     He was infested: mindful that you made him–
     (I lie: he was not mindful; had he been,
     He would have been more grateful)–but he knew
     He owed his being to you and was encouraged
     Time and again, by blessings given, to look for
     Still greater blessings; but he shunned and spurned them.
     I hardly had to call and promised nothing

Ac nulla, tamen admisit illico, audijt;   1690
Obedijt. Suadebam, honorem quaerere;
Tu temnere jubebas. Utrum secutus est?
Rogetur ipse; vicerit, si dixerit,
Semel modestiam amasse? Noctes ac dies
Quaerebat, undique ambiebat glorias.   1695
Hac fine, studia, litteras, artes bonas
Corrupit: hac fine, optimis, sanctissimis
Abusus est laboribus, quos pessimos
Effecit: hac fine, vigilavit; perdidit
Suam quietem, ut inveniret gloriam.   1700
Quid multa? talis est, ut ipse si sui
Judex sit, absolvere tamen se non velit.

SPIRITUS: Ignosce Christe, ignoscite reo Judices.

PANURGUS: Sed fecit aliqua praeclara tamen facinora;
Stipem erogavit pauperi; dubijs dedit   1705
Consilia: docuit, erudivit; profuit
Vivendo, profuit loquendo caeteris.
Haec profutura alius putet; ego non putem.
Quid enim abnuis sceleste? nunquam quiveris
Negando, facta infecta reddere. Loquitur   1710
Res ipsa: quaeque te bene agere jactitas,
Eadem male acta dicis. Adeo es perditus,
Ut neque benefacere, sine maleficio queas.
Stipem erogasti pauperi. Quando? atque ubi?
Quid conticescis? nempe vera dictito;   1715
Te turba fecit liberalem; defuit
Spectator, haud teruncium tenui dabas.
Et abstinebas a quiete. Cui rei?
Ut ne abstineres laude. Quin, si audes, nega.
Haecque impudens benefacta jactites tua?   1720
Haec digna coelo? digna Numine? Inferis
Dignissima. Nihil ut aliud peccaveris,
Bene faciendo factus es certe reus.
Haec tacta, quam dicta potius, justissime
Cognosce Judex; mihique caetera similem   1725
Simili afficito poena. Vel etenim hunc inferi
Juste asserunt, vel nos inique detinent.

CHRISTUS: Quid his super capitibus inquis? dilue
Objecta, si potes, scelera.

SPIRITUS: Parce O DEUS,

But vain and empty gifts; he listened instantly,
Heard and obeyed me. Honours I urged him seek,
You bade him scorn them. Whose bidding did he follow?
Let him be asked. He's won if he can say
That even once he courted modesty.
But day and night his single aim was glory.
For this his studies, culture, noble arts
Were all perverted; and for this the best,
The holiest means abused for basest ends.
With this in mind he kept his constant vigil.
Sleepless, he lost all peace, in quest of glory.
Need I say more? If he were his own judge,
He would not wish to absolve himself of guilt.

SPIRIT: Forgive, oh Christ; judges, forgive the accused.

PANURGUS: But he did other deeds still more renowned.
He gave alms to the poor, dispensed advice
To those in need, instructed, taught some others,
And profited the rest through word and deed.
Others may deem this profitable, not I.
Why shake your head, you sinner? Your denials
Can never make those deeds undone. The facts
Speak for themselves. All those good deeds you boast of
You can call bad. You are so lost to good,
That even your good deeds are rendered sinful.
You gave alms to the poor. But when? And where?
Why are you silent? All I say is true.
An audience made you generous. On your own
You hardly gave a needy man a farthing.
You sacrificed all rest. But to what end?
To lose no chance of praise. Dare you deny it?
Are these the deeds you boast of, shameless wretch?
The good deeds worthy of Heaven? of God? It's Hell
They merit. If you of other sins were guiltless,
Through doing good you've guaranteed your guilt.
These barely-outlined facts, most just of judges,
Be pleased to acknowledge. Like me in all else,
Punish him likewise. If the powers of Hell
Claim him unjustly, we're unjustly kept there.

CHRIST: What do you say in answer to these charges?
Lessen them if you can.

SPIRIT: Spare me, oh God,

O parce Numen. Ego per has rogo te manus,   1730
Haec per ego genua; parce supplici reo.
CHRISTUS: Absiste. Flecti nequeo misericordia;
        Olim licebat. Hunc severitas locum
        Insedit. Haec nisi diluis maleficia;
        Peristi: abito.   1735
SPIRITUS: Misericors es; flectere.
CHRISTUS: Sum justus etiam: evincere nequeunt preces
        Serae. Recede: vel refelle haec crimina.
SPIRITUS: Morulam rogo brevissimam: convellere
        Impacta possim ut crimina.
CONSCIENTIA: Quid hic expetis?
        Nunquam licebit: mille si dentur dies,   1740
        Mensesque mille, milleque anni & saecula,
        Non dilues neque unicum quidem scelus.
        Absolvat ut te Curia; tibi tu innocens
        Nunquam videberis.
SPIRITUS: Ah tamen: vel horulam.
CHRISTUS: Cum viveres, hora fuit.   1745
SPIRITUS: Etiamnum potest
        Hora esse.
CHRISTUS: Nihil agis modo.
CENODOXOPHYLAX: Has inducias
        Exoret, oro, miser; refutandi moram
        Ut habeat.
CHRISTUS: Hanc committo curam huic Curiae
        Meae. Placetne comperendinatio!
CENODOXOPHYLAX: Liceat morari.   1750
PETRUS: Nisi tamen nevis, DEUS,
        Placet.
PAULUS: Placet differre, ut aequa sentiat
        Supplicia se perferre, nisi refellerit.
CHRISTUS: Nihil moror.
CENODOXOPHYLAX: Siquid erit usquam, reperiam,
        Quod huic reo videatur adjutabile.

Spare me, oh Lord. Prostrate I beg before you,
Implore, beseech: have mercy on the accused.

CHRIST: Desist. I cannot now be moved by mercy;
Though once I could. Stern justice occupies
This judgement seat. Now wash these sins away,
Or perish. Cease.

SPIRIT: You're merciful. Be appeased.

CHRIST: I am just, and cannot be appeased by prayers
That come too late. Withdraw, or refute these charges.

SPIRIT: I ask the briefest respite, to demolish
These charges pressed against me.

CONSCIENCE: What hope have you?
There's not the slightest chance. If you were granted
A thousand days, or months, or years, or centuries,
You could not wash away a single sin.
And if the court absolved you, you could never
Find yourself innocent.

SPIRIT: A brief hour only.

CHRIST: Your hour struck while you lived.

SPIRIT: It could again
Strike for me.

CHRIST: You ask in vain.

CENODOXOPHYLAX: Grant this poor wretch,
I beg, this respite, that he may have time
To refute the charges.

CHRIST: I hand this matter over
To the assembled court. Does it agree to adjourn?

CENODOXOPHYLAX: Delay a while.

PETER: Unless, Lord, you dissent,
I agree.

PAUL: I agree to adjourn, so that the accused
May feel his judgement just, or may refute it.

CHRIST: I won't object.

CENODOXOPHYLAX: I'll see if there is anything
That may be found to help the defendant's cause.

SCENA II
CHORUS MORTUALIS, BRUNO, HUGO,
LAUDWINUS, Cum Socijs ac funere
CENODOXUS

CHORUS
  Heu, heu; flebile funus urbis; heu, heu;   1755
  Lugubrem, socij, parate lessum.
  Suum secula perdidere florem!
  Suum sidera perdidere Solem!
BRUNO: Hic collocate funus; usque dum preces
  Pro more persolvantur.——   1760
CHORUS
  Quid maesti, Cenodoxe, quid meremur,
  Aegrum linquere quod juberis orbem?
  Quo tu funere nunc humaris unus,
  Illo funere nos humamur omnes.
HUGO: Ah superstitem 1760
  Cenodoxon hunc tenere, terra, non potes: 1765
  Tene ergo functum; & nobile spolium tenes.
CHORUS
  Eheu, Curia jam cares Magistro;
  Eheu, Patria jam cares Patrono;
  Eheu, Gallia jam cares Parente;
  Eheu, Terra cares, cares salute!   1770
CENODOXUS: Heu, heu.
OMNES: DEUS serva. Quid est miraculi!
CENODOXUS: Heu, heu; verendi apud tribunal Judicis
  ACCUSATUS SUM
OMNES: Serva DEUS: parce superae Rector domus.
BRUNO: Quid audio?
HUGO: Quid sentio?
LAUDWINUS: Quid contuor?
BRUNO: Quid haec sibi novitas? Quis occupat tremor 1775
  Frigusque membra?
HUGO: Nihil animae inest corpori.
LAUDWINUS: Penissime perij: pedibus aegre meis
  Insisto.
BRUNO: Pavet animus; inhorrescunt mei
  Artus: titubat horrore lingua noxio.
  Audistis ejulantem, & horribili sono   1780
  Exclamitantem?

SCENE II
FUNERAL CHORUS, BRUNO, HUGO,
LAUDWINUS, with friends and the corpse of
CENODOXUS

CHORUS
    Ah, grievous loss! A city mourns!
    Prepare the dirge and sad lament.
    The age has lost its fairest flower!
    The stars have lost their brightest sun!
BRUNO: Set down his bier while prayers are rendered here
    According to the rites.
CHORUS
    What, Cenodoxus, have we, sad ones, done,
    That you are called to quit this ailing earth?
    With just such funeral rites as we inter you,
    With just such funerals shall we all be interred.
HUGO: You have no power,
    Oh earth, to hold a living Cenodoxus:
    Receive his body then, a noble prize.
CHORUS
    Ah, courts of justice, now gone is your master;
    Land of our fathers, now gone is your guardian;
    Gone now, oh Gaul, is your own loving father;
    Gone now, oh earth, is your safe-guard and strength!
CENODOXUS: Ah, ah.
ALL: God save us. What miracle is this?
CENODOXUS: Ah, ah; before God's fearful judgement seat
    I AM ACCUSED.
ALL: God's mercy on us; spare us, mighty Lord.
BRUNO: What do I hear?
HUGO: Or feel?
LAUDWINUS: What do I see?
BRUNO: What new portent is this? What fear, what chill
    Invades my limbs?
HUGO: All life has left my body.
LAUDWINUS: I'm almost fainting. I can hardly stand.
BRUNO: Terror invades me, and my trembling limbs
    All shake with fright. My tongue's transfixed with dread.
    Did you not hear him wail and cry out loud
    In hideous tones?

OMNES: Audivimus. Nil tetrius,
Nil horribilius anteidhac.
BRUNO: Ut extulit
Pallentia ora morte! Ut aegra lumina
Divaricavit! Ut asperis e faucibus
Extorsit illa verba?   1785
HUGO: Quid portenditis
Novitate, Superi, tam nova?
LAUDWINUS: Ergone facili
Adeo vicissitudine bona adversaque
Fortuna mortales subit? Beatior
Here nemo, quam Cenodoxus; infelicior
Hodie videtur nemo.   1790
HUGO: An accusatus est
Cenodoxus?
OMNES: Omnes perijmus, quando pereunt
Tales.
BRUNO: Perijsse non putandus ideo erit
Cenodoxus: absit, de viro integerrimo
Hoc suspicari. Nam improba Cacodaemonis
Ferenda fortasse fuit accusatio;   1795
Ut omnia solet carpere, & mendacijs
Afflare. Nam accusare quosvis, liberum est;
Damnare solos improbos. Defendere
Se novit accusata virtus.
LAUDWINUS: Quid agimus?
An ergo justa facimus? An sub alteram   1800
Hoc proferemus vesperam funus?
BRUNO: Lubet
Differre; resque videtur exigere; quoad
Eventus hujus prodigij mage liqueat.
OMNES: Placet relinqui.
BRUNO: Tu DEUS, ter maxime
Terque optime; haec portenta fac feliciter   1805
Et prospere mihi, omnibusque his accidant.

ALL: We did, and never heard
    Such dire and hideous sounds.
BRUNO: How he rose up,
    His face all pale with death! His stricken eyes
    Distended wide! And words wrenched out and forced
    From death-bound jaws!
HUGO: What, Heaven, do you portend
    By this phenomenon?
LAUDWINUS: Are mortals so
    Exposed to the vicissitudes of fortune,
    For good or ill? No-one seemed yesterday
    More blessed than Cenodoxus; and today
    No-one more wretched.
HUGO: Can he be arraigned?
ALL: If men like him are doomed, doomed are we all.
BRUNO: Such doom for Cenodoxus is unthinkable;
    Far be it from us to entertain such thoughts
    Of such a virtuous man. Perhaps the devil
    Has him arraigned on some false, trumped-up charge.
    He spreads polluting slanders everywhere.
    There's nobody who cannot be accused,
    The guilty only are convicted. Virtue
    Can fend off accusation.
LAUDWINUS: What shall we do?
    Perform the rites? Or else delay the funeral
    Until tomorrow evening?
BRUNO: Let's delay it.
    The matter seems to warrant this. Let's wait
    Until we see the outcome of this portent.
ALL: Yes, we must wait.
BRUNO: Oh God, thrice mighty one,
    Oh blessed Trinity, resolve these portents,
    And grant their outcome favour all of us.

SCENA III

CHRISTUS, D. PETRUS, D. PAULUS,
Cum Judicibus,
S. MICHAEL, CENODOXOPHYLAX, SPIRITUS CENODOXI,
CONSCIENTIA, PANURGUS

CHRISTUS: Adesse partes impera; ut reus suum
    Jus prosequatur. Arbitrabor omnia
    Ut aequitas, severitasque poposcerit.
    Clementiae hic nihil dabo.   1810
CONSCIENTIA: Haeres? Restitas?
    Sceleste; nunquam hae proderunt tibi morae.
    Ad Judicem; ad tribunal.
MICHAEL: Adsunt, Maxime
    Optimeque Judex.
SPIRITUS: Parce Christe; o Judicum
    Supreme parce.
CHRISTUS: Quanta fuerint crimina
    Impacta, quae dicta tibi scripta, intelligis.   1815
    Ad illa dicere quid habes?
PANURGUS: Obmutuit
    Nihil refellit. Ai, nega.
CONSCIENTIA: Ego pro te loquor;
    Taceas licet; jam nosceris.
SPIRITUS: Clementiam
    DEUS oro; misericordiam.
CHRISTUS: Nihil moves:
    Persisto.   1820
SPIRITUS: Per ego haec vulnera tua, per Crucem
    Necemque rogo, patere moveri.
CHRISTUS: Jam sinam
    Hinc te amoveri.
SPIRITUS: Supplicem prius vide.
CHRISTUS: Video superbiam.
SPIRITUS: Supplicem imo.
CHRISTUS: Tollite:
    Defendere nequit.
SPIRITUS: Ah, patronum aliquem mihi.
CHRISTUS: Olim dedi, & contemseras: nunc ipse age.   1825
SPIRITUS: Ah, parce Numen.
CHRISTUS: Serus es.

SCENE III

CHRIST, ST PETER, ST PAUL,
With the judges,
ST MICHAEL, CENODOXOPHYLAX, SPIRIT OF
CENODOXUS, CONSCIENCE, PANURGUS

CHRIST: Bid the two parties come, and let the accused
      Pursue his case. I shall judge everything
      According to the strict demands of justice.
      I'll show no mercy here.
CONSCIENCE: You dawdle, tarry?
      Wretch, these delays will never serve your cause.
      Now face the judge and face the court.
MICHAEL: Great judge,
      The parties are assembled.
SPIRIT: Spare me, oh Christ;
      Spare me, most mighty judge.
CHRIST: You know full well
      The charges and the deeds alleged against you.
      What answer make you to them?
PANURGUS: None at all.
      Deny them, if you dare.
CONSCIENCE: I'll speak for you.
      You need not speak; you're known already.
SPIRIT: Mercy,
      I beg, oh God. Have pity.
CHRIST: No. Unmoved
      I shall remain.
SPIRIT: By these your wounds, your Cross
      And Passion, I beseech you to be moved.
CHRIST: I'll have *you* moved.
SPIRIT: First see me humbly plead.
CHRIST: I see your pride.
SPIRIT: Humbly I plead.
CHRIST: Remove him.
      He cannot defend himself.
SPIRIT: Give me an advocate.
CHRIST: I did once, and you spurned him. Be your own.
SPIRIT: Have mercy, oh God.
CHRIST: You ask too late.

SPIRITUS: Vel infimum
  Permittito patronum.
CHRISTUS: Habere non potes.
SPIRITUS: Vel quaerere liceat.
PANURGUS: Nihil equidem veto;
  Quaerat patronos, deligat sibi Judices.
  Nemo hunc tueri quibit.   1830
SPIRITUS: Ah siqua miseri
  Miseratio te tangit, hic opem tuo
  Praebe clienti.
MICHAEL: Tu cliens meus? apage.
SPIRITUS: Cliens, profecto.
MICHAEL: Hostis: clientem nescio.
SPIRITUS: Ego saepe te multumque colui.
MICHAEL: Men' scelus?
SPIRITUS: Te.   1835
MICHAEL: Te colueras: cede; nil tibi est opis.
SPIRITUS: Ah tamen.
MICHAEL: Ego arrogantiam proscribere
  Soleo: patrocinor superbo nemini.
  Abi.
SPIRITUS: At mihi tu opitulare Princeps aetheris
  Claviger.
PETRUS: Abi.
SPIRITUS: Meminisse potes etiam tibi
  Idem periculum fuisse, cum DEUM   1840
  Negando laeseras?
PETRUS: Probe memini equidem,
  Factumque damno.
SPIRITUS: Tunc tamen tu flectere
  Numen potis eras.
PETRUS: Lacrimis potui meis
  In tempore profusis: fuissem serior,
  Tecum fuissem. Tolle te hinc; me non moves.   1845
SPIRITUS: Te vero, te per quicquid est sanctum est tibi,
  Obtestor; admitte miserum.
PAULUS: Hic aeque parum
  Extundis. Absiste; actum agis: nihil impetras.
CONSCIENTIA: Huc huc, sceleste; ego te tuebor: lumina
  Huc verte, conscientiam vide tuam.   1850
  Te posse defendi negat, quamvis velis,
  Velintque tecum, quotquot usquam victitant.

SPIRIT: But grant me
        The meanest advocate.
CHRIST: You can have none.
SPIRIT: Then let me look for one.
PANURGUS: I'll not oppose.
        Let him seek advocates and choose his judges.
        None can defend him.
SPIRIT: If you are touched by pity
        For my sad plight, then grant your client aid.
MICHAEL: My client? You? Be off!
SPIRIT: Your client indeed.
MICHAEL: My enemy, you mean, no client.
SPIRIT: I often
        Did greatly venerate you.
MICHAEL: What me, you sinner?
SPIRIT: Yes, you.
MICHAEL: Yourself you worshipped. Go–unaided.
SPIRIT: Forbear.
MICHAEL: I outlaw arrogance and never
        Defend the proud. Go now.
SPIRIT: Oh heavenly prince
        And keeper of the keys, assist me now.
PETER: Begone.
SPIRIT: Can you remember your own peril,
        When by denying God you wounded Him?
PETER: I do remember, and condemn my deed.
SPIRIT: And yet you made God merciful to you.
PETER: My tears accomplished this, shed in good time.
        Had I repented late, I would have been
        Like you arraigned. Be off. You'll not move me.
SPIRIT: By all your holiness I call on you;
        Help me in need.
PAUL: No, you'll extort no more
        From me. Desist. You're done for. You'll gain nothing.
CONSCIENCE: Look here, wretch. I shall guard you. Turn your eyes
        And gaze on me, your conscience. Conscience says
        There's no defence for you, however much
        You, and all those who live on earth, may wish it.

SPIRITUS: O magna spes, o una mea fiducia,
    Supplex tibi accido.
CENODOXOPHYLAX: Citius modo feceras,
    Non defuissem. Ah sero, sero, consulis.   1855
SPIRITUS: Adeone supplicem tuum tu respuis!
CENODOXOPHYLAX: Ego saepe supplex ipse fiebam tibi;
    Rogabam, & obsecrabam ut admittere mea
    Consilia velles; respuisti me tamen.
SPIRITUS: Vel jam tuere, qua potes.   1860
CHRISTUS: Defendere
    Hunc posse tibi videris?
CENODOXOPHYLAX: Innocentior
    Si foret. At innocentiam hanc frustra vovet.
    Suppeditat accusatio mihi plurima,
    Nulla penitus defensio. Adversarius
    Quaecunque dixit, vera dixit, cum meo   1865
    Dolore. Librum hunc intuor? vitia intuor
    Merissima, & gravissima, & grandissima.
    Scrutatus omnia, sicubi levissimum
    Vestigium virtutis animadverterem;
    Nihil actitavi. Evanidae sunt litterae   1870
    Quaedam super; Precationis, & Stipis:
    Sed has Superbiae atque Hypocriseos lues
    Induxit ipsas. Arrogantia undique
    Et undique legitur. Monebam clanculo
    Palamque, noctes & dies, faceret uti   1875
    Modum superbiae; superbijt magis
    Et peior e correctionibus meis
    Occoepit esse. Terrui per somnia,
    Acheruntaque ipsos posui ob oculos. Somnia
    Sed illa risit, sprevit, ac ludibrio   1880
    Habuit. Suprema cum diem necessitas
    Urgeret, adfui; juvare promtior
    Quam ipse adjuvari. Respuit; dictis fidem
    Nullam habuit, exclusit; inimicos audijt
    Meos suosque. Nihil omisi ut vincerem   1885
    Tam saxeum pectus. Sed hoc profeceram,
    Ut cernerem effectum nihil. Poteras meos
    Ita tu labores spernere improbe? ita tuam
    Temnere salutem? prodigus vitae & animae,
    Animam secundum gloriam tu ducere?   1890

SPIRIT: Oh my great hope, my one sure trust, I beg
     And crave your help.
CENODOXOPHYLAX: If you had asked me sooner,
     I would have helped you. Ah! you ask too late!
SPIRIT: You spurn your ward when he implores your aid?
CENODOXOPHYLAX: I often went on bended knee to you.
     I begged, besought you to listen to my advice
     And follow it. But still you cast me off.
SPIRIT: Yet help me where you can.
CHRIST: And do you think
     You can defend this man?
CENODOXOPHYLAX: Had he but been
     More innocent! But this he pleads in vain.
     Charges against him I can bring in plenty,
     Nothing in his defence. The prosecutor
     Spoke nothing but the truth, to my great sorrow.
     I look into this book and see his sins,
     Nothing but sins, most grave, appalling sins.
     I scan each single page, hoping to find
     The merest trace or slightest hint of virtue.
     My efforts are in vain. Occasionally
     Some scholarly ephemera, prayers, some alms.
     Even these corrupt hypocrisy and pride
     Corroded. Everywhere on every page
     The word pride is writ large. Both night and day
     I warned him secretly and openly
     To curb his pride. He gloried in it more,
     Going from bad to worse, try as I would
     To better him. I conjured up dire dreams,
     With nightmare sights of hell. He spurned them all,
     Laughed them to scorn, rejected them with ridicule.
     When came his fatal hour, I was at hand;
     More prompt to help, than he was to be helped.
     He cast me out, believed no word I said,
     Excluded me–and heard my enemies,
     My enemies and his. I tried all means
     To win his stony heart. All I achieved
     Was knowledge of my failure. Could you so
     Despise my efforts, sinner? So disdain
     Your own salvation? Squander life and soul,
     Rating your soul below your worldly glory?

Tu sidera adeo nauseare! tu solum,
Solique honores aetheri anteponere?
Tu Numen orco posthabere? Caelites
Ita fugere? Stygios ita hostes quaerere?
I nunc, eosdem opta Patronos. Qui mea   1895
Nunquam usus es ope olim, nec uteris etiam
Modo, cum voles. Jam jus tibi renuntio
Vetus Patroni. Cede: prodesse nequeo,
Neque volo.

SPIRITUS: Deseresne alumnum in ultimo
Discrimine capitis?   1900

CENODOXOPHYLAX: Prior me tu iveras
Desertum.

SPIRITUS: At hic reverto.

CENODOXOPHYLAX: Itane? dum vivitur,
Dum fors secunda spirat, & felicitas
Dominatur, & dum absunt procul pericula,
Adestque gloria, Genios contemnitis
Bonos; sequentes fugitis usque; & obvios   1905
Cavetis usque; & praevios relinquitis;
Comites abigitis; servientes unice
Vestrae saluti luditis & excluditis.
Monemus, obsurdescitis: jubemus &
Hortamur, abnuitis: rogamus, pergitis: 1910
Blandimur, horretis: minamur, spernitis:
Terremus, obdurescitis: compellimus,
Resistitis: vocamus, aspernamini:
Revocamus, exsecramini: bene facimus,
Malefacitis: monstramus & promittimus   1915
Coelestia, improbatis: agimus omnia,
Abnuitis omnia. Quando vero calamitas
Tandem appetit suprema, tunc alumnuli
Vos esse nostri; tunc item clientulos
Vos nominare; Nos patronos dicere,   1920
Rogare, supplicare, asylum credere:
Exigere jus fidemque Tutelarium,
Cum vos tamen jus & fidem clientium
Neglexeritis. Ergo usque adeo patientiam
Contemnitis nostram? Salutem nos quoque   1925
Hic negligemus vestram. Abi ergo, & desine
Rogare.

Reject the realms of light with such disgust,
Holding earth's glories higher than those of heaven?
Esteem God less than hell? And so renounce
The angelic throng and court the hosts of Satan?
Go, choose them as your guardians, you who never
Used my help then, shall never use it now,
Though now you want it. I my sacred patronage
Do now renounce. Desist. I cannot help you,
And I will not.

SPIRIT: Do you desert your ward
In direst need?

CENODOXOPHYLAX: You first deserted me.

SPIRIT: I now turn back to you.

CENODOXOPHYLAX: At such a time!
When you're alive and fortune smiles on you,
Contentment reigns, all perils far removed,
And glory beckons, you despise good angels,
Shun our attentions, block our every entrance,
And leave us when we try to show the way;
Avoid our company and mock and block
Those who strive only for your soul's salvation.
We warn you, you grow deaf; command, exhort you,
And you refuse us; beg, and you persist.
You bristle at blandishments, and scoff at threats;
We give you fearful warnings: you grow hard;
Compulsion makes you stubborn, you spurn our summons;
Call you again, you curse; do good to you,
You sin; we show the way to promised heaven,
And you despise it; we urge with all persuasions,
And all are spurned. But when your last calamity
Finally overtakes you, you become
Our little nurslings; call yourselves our clients;
Speak to us as your guardian patrons, plead
And humbly beg, expecting our protection,
Demanding all your rights and dues as wards,
When all our rights and dues as guardians
You have disdained. Is this how you despise
Our patient care? We too shall disregard
Your soul's salvation. Go, and cease to plead.

SPIRITUS: Perij.

PANURGUS: Sero sentis; senseram
          Perisse dudum. Caeterum justissime
          Judex, vides non posse defendi reum;
          Superest, secundum me tuam ut pronunties   1930
          Sententiam.

CHRISTUS: Tu vera dicis crimina
          Haec esse ?

SPIRITUS: Non tam gravia rebar.

CONSCIENTIA: Decipit:
          Sciebat. Aeternis ego movere stimulis
          Non destiti. Saepe anxium, & rebus suis
          Subinde diffidentem adorta presseram.   1935
          Hoc saepe judicium oculis objeceram;
          Sed tanta laudis cupiditas illum fuit
          Amplexa, tanta plebis aestimatio,
          Ut ferre morsus perpetes assueverit,
          Dum ferre laudem posset: ut contemnere   1940
          Hoc Numinis terribile Judicium sui
          Assueverit, dum judicia mortalium
          Magni aestimaret. Haec loquor; silentium
          Mihi imperari non sino: tacens audior.

SPIRITUS: Ah parce Numen.   1945

CHRISTUS: Nullus es.

SPIRITUS: Parce optime
          Parens.

CHRISTUS: Peristi.

SPIRITUS: Per ego te tuos rogo
          Vitae labores.

CHRISTUS: Abstine.

SPIRITUS: Per vulnera.

CHRISTUS: Frustra es.

SPIRITUS: Per hanc ego te crucem tuam obsecro.

CHRISTUS: Omitte.

SPIRITUS: Per necem.

CHRISTUS: Actum agis.

SPIRITUS: Vos vero, vos
          Flectite rigorem hunc Judices.   1950

MICHAEL: Nil gratiae
          Datur hic nocenti.

SPIRITUS: Supplicis miseremini,
          Servate perditum.

SPIRIT: Then I am doomed.

PANURGUS: Too late you realise that.
   I've long known you are doomed. Most just of judges,
   You see that the accused has no defence.
   Nothing remains but that you judge him mine.

CHRIST: Do you admit these sins are true?

SPIRIT: Their gravity
   I did not know.

CONSCIENCE: He lies; he knew it well.
   Unceasingly, relentlessly I stung him.
   Most frequently I filled him with anxiety,
   And often shook his trust in his affairs.
   Often I made him see this judgement seat;
   But such a lust for praise had filled his heart,
   Such a desire for popular esteem,
   That he became inured to all my pangs,
   As long as all men praised him, grew accustomed
   Contemptuously to regard God's dreadful judgment,
   While glorying in the judgements of mere mortals.
   This I declare, nor shall I be compelled
   To silence. Even silence pleads my cause.

SPIRIT: Have mercy!

CHRIST: You are lost.

SPIRIT: Most loving father,
   Spare me.

CHRIST: You are condemned.

SPIRIT: I beg, beseech you
   By all your toilsome life.

CHRIST: Cease.

SPIRIT: By your wounds.

CHRIST: In vain.

SPIRIT: By this your Cross I do beseech you.

CHRIST: Refrain.

SPIRIT: And by your death.

CHRIST: Your cause is lost.

SPIRIT: You judges, mitigate this rigorous sentence.

MICHAEL: The guilty find no grace here.

SPIRIT: Ah! Have mercy,
   Save my lost soul.

PETRUS: Facesse jam hinc preces.
PAULUS: Serae preces, quas hoc loci facit reus.
    Alibi has oportuit.
CONSCIENTIA: Tibi sententia
    Scribenda si foret, ipse te haud absolveres.   1955
    Quid ergo speres ab alijs defendier?
CHRISTUS: Nihil opus est sententijs: una omnium
    Mens, atque vox; *Reum videri.*
OMNES: Noxius
    Cenodoxus est; reus, improbus Cenodoxus est.

SCENA IV
BRUNO, LAUDWINUS, HUGO, Cum Socijs,
CHORUS MORTUALIS, CENODOXUS

BRUNO: Nox pervigil abijt mihi omnis, & diem   1960
    Dum expecto, credidi esse paene saeculum.
    Ita me attonuit hesterna nostri funeris
    Formido.
LAUDWINUS: Visamus, quod heri reliquimus,
    Ad corpus, atque justa solvamus hodie.
CHORUS MORTUALIS
    Heu quam terribile est, cernere Numinis   1965
    Armatam trifido fulmine dexteram?
    Iratumque minas spargere judicem?
      Et paenas scelerum lege reposcere?
    Quin tandem vitijs mittite nuntios;
    Ac tam luctifico funere territi,   1970
    Vobis tam rigidum pergite pergite
      Armatis precibus flectere Judicem.
CENODOXUS: Ah, ah. Severum apud tribunal Numinis,
    JUSTO DEI JUDICIO JUDICATUS SUM.
OMNES: O superum hominumque fidem: quid hoc? miraculum   1975
    Redintegratur.
BRUNO: Denuo caput extulit
    Informe!
HUGO: Judicatus ergo a Numine
    Cenodoxus? ipseque praeco judicij sui?
    O Tristem visu; o lugubrem catastrophen!
LAUDWINUS: DEUS! quid haec sibi volunt teterrima   1980

PETER: Have done now with these prayers.

PAUL: Prayers here made by the accused are prayers too late.
They should have been made elsewhere.

CONSCIENCE: Had you now
To judge yourself, you'd not acquit yourself.
Why therefore look to others to defend you?

CHRIST: It is not necessary to sound opinions.
We all are of one mind and voice: *he's guilty*.

ALL: Guilty is evil, godless Cenodoxus.

SCENE IV
BRUNO, LAUDWINUS, HUGO, and companions,
FUNERAL CHORUS, CENODOXUS

BRUNO: I've passed a sleepless night; the leaden hours
While I awaited dawn have seemed an age,
I was so anguished by those obsequies
And by that dread event.

LAUDWINUS: Let us revisit
The body and fulfil the abandoned rites.

FUNERAL CHORUS
Ah with what fear do we see the heaven's Mighty One,
Armed with the thunderbolt, flash his right hand;
Speak in his anger the harsh words of judgement,
Visit the sinner with penalties just!
Cease then your sinfulness, turn from all evil,
Terror-struck grieving this soul-searing death;
Plead without ceasing to heaven's stern arbiter,
Beg the stern judge to be merciful yet.

CENODOXUS: Ah, ah, before heaven's rigorous tribunal
JUDGEMENT IS PASSED ON ME BY GOD'S JUST
JUDGEMENT.

ALL: By all the powers of heaven and earth! The marvel
Repeats itself.

BRUNO: Again he lifted up
His hideous head!

HUGO: Has God judged Cenodoxus?
And is he thus announcing his own doom?
Oh dire catastrophe, sad spectacle!

LAUDWINUS: Oh God, what do these sights and horrors mean?

Spectacula, an miracula? Mihin' mortui
Vox vera sonuit? tamque dira nuntiat
Mortalibus de rebus immortalibus?

BRUNO: Horresco pristini memor adhuc funeris,
 Et jam novo auget horror antiquus metu.   1985
 Audire non tam mortuum, quam mortuus
 Loqui ipse videor.

HUGO: Supplicemus Numini
 Hac nocte; & iram molliamus Judicis,
 Siqua impiatus fortean migraverit
 Cenodoxus orbe.   1990

BRUNO: Differamus interim
 Tumulare corpus.

LAUDWINUS: Atqui judicatus est;
 Quid proderis?

BRUNO: Nec vero constat undique
 Quae judicij fuerit peracta formula.
 Innoxios quoque judicare dicimur,
 Cum absolvimus. Cenodoxus ergo absolvitur 1995
 Fortasse judicatus; aut incendio
 Piaculari urgetur.

OMNES: Ergo haec alterum
 Res differatur in diem.

BRUNO: Quae tempora
 Incidimus? eheu vivimus, nec vivimus:
 Morique cogimur, neque sinimur mori.   2000

SCENA V
CHRISTUS, Cum reliquis Judicibus,
SPIRITUS CENODOXI, PANURGUS

CHRISTUS: Revocate; producite scelestum: ut ultimo
 Hinc jure proscribatur; aevitatibus
 Arsurus omnibus.

OMNES: Satis diu hactenus
 Impune scelerato fuit.

CHRISTUS: Adesdum scelus;
 Et digna factis accipe tuis praemia.   2005

SPIRITUS: Saevire noli, o Judicum mitissime.

CHRISTUS: Quae te libido praecipitem in hanc compulit

And did I truly hear a dead man's voice?
And did he so announce to mortal men
Dire tidings of immortal mysteries?

BRUNO: I shudder still since those first obsequies;
Now horror heightens all that fear anew.
I hear a dead man speak; or it seems rather
As if I am a corpse myself and speak.

HUGO: Let's spend this night in prayer, beseeching God
To curb and soften his judicial wrath
Lest, sin-stained, Cenodoxus quit this earth.

BRUNO: Defer the burial.

LAUDWINUS: What good is that?
He has been judged.

BRUNO: We cannot yet be sure
What form of judgement has been passed on him.
We also say the innocent are judged
When we acquit them. Cenodoxus too
May be adjudged acquitted; or be beset
By purging fire.

ALL: So let us put it off
Another day.

BRUNO: What times are come upon us!
We live, alas, and yet we do not live;
We are driven to death but not allowed to die.

SCENE V
CHRIST, with the other judges,
SPIRIT OF CENODOXUS, PANURGUS

CHRIST: Summon the sinner back, that final judgement
May be pronounced on him: that he shall burn
For all succeeding ages.

ALL: Long enough
His sins have gone unpunished.

CHRIST: Sinner, stay!
Receive your evil doings' just deserts.

SPIRIT: Oh spare your wrath, most merciful of judges.

CHRIST: What fond desire possessed you, drove you headlong

Vesaniam, sceleste; Numen ut tuum
Contemneres? hostisque profugeres mei
Ad castra? quo maleficio te laeseram?   2010
Quo te beneficio hostis affecit meus?
Ineamus, ingrate, rationem. Condidi
Te, cum cinis, pulvis, nihilque esses, mea
Ut imperata facere sic assuesceres.
Sed tibi nefando pestifera placuit sequi   2015
Consilia veteratoris, exclusis meis.
Nec vero spretus benefacere tibi desij;
Caepique magis amare, quo tu me oderas
Magis: parumque facere me putaveram,
Nisi nimium facerem. Ideoque sidera   2020
Deserueram, ut tu sidera coleres: humum
Ideo colebam, ut tu relinqueres humum.
Contemsi honores, ut meo contemneres
Exemplo honores. Te meum jejunium
Dolebat; atque vigiliae tibi meae   2025
Quondam excubabant. Te meis laboribus
Itineribusque perditum quaesiveram;
Et cum sim ubique, nuspiam te repereram.
Injurias & contumelias tui
Amore sustinui; esseque odio plurimis   2030
Non horrui, dum te quasi unicum unice
Amare possem. Verbera, flagra corpore
Innoxio, pro noxio te pertuli.
Crucem necemque subij, ut exires tuam.
Has testor ipse manus, pedesque vulnere   2035
Consauciatos: haec tropea, hosce cuneos;
Quae cuncta contueris hic praesentia.
Loquatur universa terrae machina;
Loquatur universa caeli Curia;
Majora me nequijsse ponere merita,   2040
Nec debuisse; dummodo ego temet mihi
Tibique memet dedicatum obstringerem.
Sed esse tanto alienior, quo charior
Occoeperas; meritaque delictis mea
Pariare vel superare quam creberrimis   2045
Frustra volebas. Arrogantia meam
Submissionem vincere; & modestiam
Superbia; candorem hypocrisi; bona

Into such madness, wretched sinner, that
You set your God at naught? Took refuge in
My enemy's camp? What injury have I done you?
What favour has my enemy bestowed?
Let's draw the reckoning up, ungrateful wretch.
I gave you being when you were ashes, dust,
Were nothing, formed you to do all my bidding.
But, sinful, you preferred the baneful counsels
Of the arch enemy, ignoring mine.
Though spurned, I still remained your benefactor.
The more you hated me, the more my love
Grew for you, fearing I had done too little,
Unless I did too much. So I descended
From heaven that you might live in heaven; I lived
On earth to enable you to leave the earth.
Honours I scorned, that following my example
You might scorn honours. For you I fasted, sorrowed,
For you I passed the sleepless nights in vigil,
Kept constant watch. And you were the lost sheep
I journeyed after, sought in all my labours.
Yet I, though everywhere, could find you nowhere.
For love of you I bore the wrongs, the affronts;
And shrank not from the hatred of the many
As long as I could count you my one love.
I suffered all the blows and scourging stripes
Upon my sinless body, for sinful you.
Death and the cross I bore, freeing you from death.
By these my hands, my wounded, ravaged feet
I testify, these instruments and trophies,
Which you behold arrayed before you here.
Let the whole fabric of the earth proclaim,
And let the entire celestial host proclaim:
No greater services could I perform,
No more should I have needed to perform,
To bind you fast to me and me to you.
You turned from me the more, the more I loved you.
You vainly sought to equal all my blessings
Or to outdo them by repaying them
With frequent sinful deeds. Your arrogance
Defeated my humility, your pride
My candour, your hypocrisy my trust,

Malis. Ego superbiam olim non tuli
Caelituum inultam; tun' tuam ferri putes?   2050
I, digna lue supplicia; patere perpetes
Per omnis aevitatis omnes terminos
Flammas paratas daemoni malo. Quibus
Lamenta, dentiumque stridor perpetim
Exaudientur: inde nulla aeternitas   2055
Eripiet.
SPIRITUS: Heu, heu, heu; Cadite montes super
Me, obruiteque una.
OMNES JUDICES: Justa judicia DEI.
Pereat scelestus.
PANURGUS: Captus es; meus es; eris;
Nec esse desines.
SPIRITUS: Pereat utinam dies,
Pereatque quisquis fecit, & vidit diem.   2060

SCENA VI
BRUNO, LAUDWINUS, HUGO, Cum Socijs,
CENODOXUS

BRUNO: Cum horrore redeo ad funus hoc, unde toties
Cum horrore abivi.
LAUDWINUS: Utinam haec secundos exitus
Prodigia sortiantur.
HUGO: Utinam. Sed modo
Ad funus instaurandum adeste; & ultimum
Cenodoxo honorem habete; si tamen licet.   2065
CENODOXUS: Heu me, heu miserrimum omnium; heu, heu, heu.
OMNES: DEUS!
O Christe?
CENODOXUS: Mittite, mittite istas, mittite
Nil profuturas postmodum exequias. Mihi
Nequitis ultra adminiculari. Perierit,
Utinam perierit mater illa, quae edidit   2070
Infausta me; o miserum! o miserrimumque me
                              Mortalium.   2072
JUSTO DEI JUDICIO DAMNATUS SUM.
Perennes eheu jam rogos   2073
Passurus abeo.

Your evil deeds my good. I did not suffer
The arrogance of angels unavenged;
Shall I now suffer yours? Then undergo
Your proper punishment: from age to age
To endure the flames prepared for the arch fiend.
Gnashing of teeth and wailing shall be heard
Perpetually; and no eternity
Shall snatch you from there.

SPIRIT: Ah! Let mountains fall
And bury me.

ALL THE JUDGES: Let him for ever perish
Through God's just judgement.

PANURGUS: You're my captive, mine,
And shall be evermore.

SPIRIT: Cursed be this day,
Accursed whoever made, whoever saw it.

SCENE VI
BRUNO, LAUDWINUS, HUGO, with companions,
CENODOXUS

BRUNO: This corpse which I have left so often in fear
In fear I now return to.

LAUDWINUS: May a good ending
Attend these wondrous portents.

HUGO: May that be so.
But let the funeral rites proceed: God willing,
We'll pay the final honours to Cenodoxus.

CENODOXUS: Ah me! Most wretched of all men!

ALL: Oh God!
Oh Christ!

CENODOXUS: Leave off these funeral obsequies,
These prayers. They cannot help me any more.
Nothing you do can help. May she be cursed,
Be cursed, that ill-starred mother who brought me forth!
Ah wretched me, most miserable of men!
BY GOD'S JUST JUDGEMENT I AM ETERNALLY
    DAMNED.
Ah me, now I depart to suffer flames
And everlasting fires.

OMNES: Parce, parce Numinis
    Severa dextra.   2075
LAUDWINUS: Perijmus, ni judicas
    Punisque mitius scelera mortalium.
BRUNO: Ah quid animi est perituro?
HUGO: Quid putem
    Quondam futurum me misello?
LAUDWINUS: Deficit
    Animus timore.
BRUNO: Vivere aeque displicet
    Morique.   2080
OMNES: Quo fugimus? Quid agimus?
BRUNO: An uspiam haec
    Judicia declinabimus?
HUGO: Quid lacrimae
    Moramini? quin prosilitis? Judicem
    In tempore ut flectatis?
LAUDWINUS: Humescant genae,
    Madeantque diffluantque fletu pectora,
    Nec fessa fletu, flere lumina desinant,   2085
    Dum parcat ille Judicum rigidissimus.
BRUNO: Hic Numen ure, caede, plecte, seca, feri,
    Saevi; nihil relinquito hic cruciatuum,
    Ut alibi parcas.
LAUDWINUS: O DEI recondita
    Sensa! Quis enim pronuper usquam sanctior   2090
    Cenodoxo erat habitus? quis innocentior?
    Sed illa sanctitas, & innocentia
    Apud severi Judicis subsellia
    Nec sanctitas fuit, nec innocentia.
BRUNO: Relinquo dirum funus; & qui nescio   2095
    Succurrere alteri, mihi ipsi consulam.

SCENA VII
PANURGUS, ASTEROTH, ASEMPHOLOTH,
HYPOCRISIS, PHILAUTIA, SPIRITUS CENODOXI

PANURGUS: Ha ha; quid horres? inter alienos tibi
        Videris esse? noster es; tui sumus.
SPIRITUS: Hostes mei estis.

ALL: Have mercy, God.
    Be sparing in your judgement.
LAUDWINUS: We all are doomed
    Unless you judge the sins of men more mildly.
BRUNO: What is the fate of the soul damned?
HUGO: And what
    May sometime be my own unhappy fate?
LAUDWINUS: My heart is faint with dread.
BRUNO: Both life and death
    Appal me equally.
ALL: Where can we go?
    What do?
BRUNO: Or how escape such dreadful judgements?
HUGO: Tears, why so slow? Why not gush forth and soften
    The judge's heart now?
LAUDWINUS: Let our cheeks grow moist,
    Our hearts dissolve, suffused with copious weeping,
    Our eyes, though worn with tears, not cease to flow,
    If that most stern of judges but grant mercy.
BRUNO: Burn, strike and lash, oh God, and vent your wrath,
    And spare no pain or torture in this world
    That in the next we may be saved.
LAUDWINUS: How dark
    God's judgements are. For who was ever thought
    More saintly and innocent than Cenodoxus?
    But this his sanctity and innocence
    Before the judgement seat of that stern judge
    Was neither sanctity nor innocence.
BRUNO: I leave this ominous corpse; and being unable
    To save another, seek my own salvation.

SCENE VII
PANURGUS, ASTEROTH, ASEMPHOLOTH,
HYPOCRISY, SELF-LOVE, THE SPIRIT OF CENODOXUS

PANURGUS: Ha, ha. Why shudder so? Do you imagine
    You're among enemies? You're ours; we're yours.
SPIRIT: You are my enemies.

ASTEROTH: Hospites imo tui.
ASEMPHOLOTH: Quid jam ferocis? placidior fueras heri.   2100
SPIRITUS: Impostor es.
ASEMPHOLOTH: Pridem sciebas; cur fidem
      Tamen habuisti?
SPIRITUS: Non habebo in posterum.
OMNES: Cenodoxe salve.
SPIRITUS: Salvus esse desij.
      Perij.
PANURGUS: Perire non potes.
SPIRITUS: Perij.
ASTEROTH: Vales,
      Valebis.   2105
SPIRITUS: Heu, perij.
PANURGUS: Medebor ocyus;
      Jam senties te non perisse: Poculum hoc
      Haurito.
SPIRITUS: Potitare jam nihil lubet.
OMNES: Ho, ho; lubere nostra debent.
PANURGUS: Hauries:
      Inverge.
SPIRITUS: Male sit mortualibus; male
      Superis & inferis.   2110
PHILAUTIA: Ut istaec potio
      Sapuit?
SPIRITUS: Male sit & tibi, lues, pestis mea.
HYPOCRISIS: Ne tu ita resiste: noscis Hypocrisin tuam?
SPIRITUS: Male tibi, Hypocrisis; Philautiae male.
      Parentibus male sit meis; rebus male
      Sit omnibus.   2115
ASTEROTH: Quam bella comprecatio!
HYPOCRISIS: Divina: nam divinus est.
PANURGUS: Advertere
      Novit suum egregie animum ad nostrum.
ASTEROTH: Bene
      Docilis es ingenij.
PHILAUTIA: Potissimus fuit,
      Nempe, omnium & prudentium & sapientium.
HYPOCRISIS: Quasi corculum & prudentiae & sapientiae.   2120
PANURGUS: Antistes ergo litteris creabitur
      Phlegethonticis.

ASTEROTH: No, we're your hosts.

ASEMPHOLOTH: Why now so fierce? you were calmer yesterday.

SPIRIT: You're a deceiver.

ASEMPHOLOTH: You knew that long ago.
　　Why did you trust us then?

SPIRIT: I won't in future.

ALL: Hail Cenodoxus!

SPIRIT: I'm no longer hale.
　　I'm finished.

PANURGUS: You can't be finished.

SPIRIT: I'm finished.

ASTEROTH: You're well,
　　And will get better.

SPIRIT: I'm finished.

PANURGUS: I'll cure you quickly.
　　You'll soon feel you're not finished. Drain this glass.

SPIRIT: I don't want any drink.

ALL: Ho, ho. You have
　　To want our drinks.

PANURGUS: Now drink up; toss it back.

SPIRIT: A curse on all the human race. A curse
　　On heaven and hell.

SELF-LOVE: Did it taste good, that drink?

SPIRIT: A curse on you, you plague, you ruined me.

HYPOCRISY: Don't be so stubborn. I'm your Hypocrisy.
　　Remember me?

SPIRIT: Be cursed. Self-Love, be cursed.
　　A curse on both my parents. And let all things
　　Be cursed.

ASTEROTH: What charming prayers indeed!

HYPOCRISY: Divine!
　　But now he is divine.

PANURGUS: It's quite remarkable
　　How he adapts his ways to ours.

ASTEROTH: Well done!
　　You do learn quickly.

SELF-LOVE: Well, he was the ablest
　　Of all the very wisest, cleverest men.

HYPOCRISY: The very fount of wisdom and of learning.

PANURGUS: Why then, we'll make him Dean of Liberal Studies
　　In fiery hell.

SPIRITUS: Male litteris; & artibus
          Male universis.
HYPOCRISIS: Hinc tibi tamen gloriam
          Tu comparasti!
SPIRITUS: Ah, comparavi miseriam.
ASTEROTH: Pollere consilijs solebat; Lucifer   2125
          Meus Imperator, illius egebit opera.
PANURGUS: Perenne protinus dabit salarium.
PHILAUTIA: Quam tu beatus?
SPIRITUS: Quam miser?
PHILAUTIA: Nescis tuam
          Beatitatem.
SPIRITUS: Heu, nescio miser, nescio.
PANURGUS: Jam jam scies.   2130
ASEMPHOLOTH: Cruciantur inferi mora;
          Expectat Imperator; atque dexterum
          Avet hunc recipere sessum, honoris gratia.
SPIRITUS: Male sit honori.
OMNES: Agite, rapite; praeducite
          Ad inferorum aeterna domicilia.
SPIRITUS: Solum
          Caelumque, quicquid uspiam est, pereat male.   2135
PANURGUS: Cadaver evolvamus itidem huc in lutum
          Caenumque, donec Orcus illud asserat.

SCENA VIII
BRUNO, Cum sex Socijs,
HUGONE, LAUDWINO, GUARINO,
STEPHANO, PHILARETO, ANDREA,
Choro

BRUNO: Nihil est necesse, credo, multis dicere,
          Cur vos potissimum evocarim. Nam docet
          Loquiturque caussam, me tacente, mortui   2140
          Vox viva: quae me vosque noctes ac dies
          Terrefacit; inque gaudijs gaudia negat:
          Suamque metuit vita vitam; animum animus:
          Suspecta sunt, quaecunque sunt. Molestiam
          Creant amoena; & inopiam faciunt opes.   2145
          Tormenta deliciae novant; premitque spem

SPIRIT: A curse on liberal studies
        And all the arts.
HYPOCRISY: But it was from the arts
        You gained your glory!
SPIRIT: Gained my wretchedness.
ASTEROTH: He used to be a most esteemed adviser:
        My master Lucifer will make good use of him.
PANURGUS: Keep him employed for all eternity.
SELF-LOVE: How blessed you are!
SPIRIT: How wretched!
SELF-LOVE: You don't know
        Your blessedness.
SPIRIT: Alas, I don't, I don't.
PANURGUS: You soon will know.
ASEMPHOLOTH: Hell brooks no more delay.
        Our lord and master waits to greet this soul,
        And seat him on his right–*honoris causa*.
SPIRIT: Cursed be this honour.
ALL: Up now, bear him off,
        Take him to his eternal home in hell.
SPIRIT: Cursed be the sun, the sky and all creation.
PANURGUS: Let's roll him over in this mud and mire
        Until hell claims his carcase as its own.

SCENE VIII
BRUNO, with six companions,
HUGO, LAUDWINUS, GUARINUS,
STEPHANUS, PHILARETUS, ANDREAS,
And Chorus

BRUNO: I need not say, I think, with many words
        Why I have called you here. Though I were silent,
        The dead expressively proclaims the reason
        With living voice–that voice which haunts with horror
        Our nights and days; turns joy to joylessness.
        Life fears its very life; mind rends the mind,
        And all that is, is suspect. Dull disgust
        Is pleasure's end; riches are no enrichment.
        Delights are racked with torment, hope is choked

　　　　Timor perennis. Esitare, litteris
　　　　Vacare, disputare, legere, colloqui
　　　　Cenodoxus arcet: dormientem me excitat;
　　　　Vigilem exanimat: adest mihi, quoties abest.　　　　2150
　　　　Quid multa? vivere, prohibet; terret, mori.
STEPHANUS: Obsedit idem luctus & animum meum,
　　　　Bruno; sed anceps consilij, quid ordiar
　　　　Ignoro.
ANDREAS:　　Suade, Bruno, siquid suppetit.
BRUNO: Pacare meque vosque statui. Vivere　　　　2155
　　　　In his periculis, ubi alios viderim
　　　　Perijsse, taedet.
OMNES:　　　　　　　Omnibus inest taedium hoc
　　　　Idem: deest medela.
BRUNO:　　　　　　　　Socij, novimus
　　　　Qua sanctitate, quaque virtute fuerit
　　　　Vitam agere visus, ille, quem modo vidimus　　　　2160
　　　　Supplicia luere apud stygem extremissima.
OMNES: Hoc ipse nobis dixit audientibus.
ANDREAS: Quam caussam oportet hujus esse?
BRUNO:　　　　　　　　　　　Utinam, utinam
　　　　Disertius caussam addidisset? ilicet
　　　　Fugeremus illam; & quicquid illum perdidit,　　　　2165
　　　　Nos perderemus. Sed profecto clarius
　　　　Caussam tacendo dixit; & salubrius
　　　　Ita supprimendo expressit. Odium diceret
　　　　Caussam fuisse? Nos etiam odium statim
　　　　Excluderemus; alia crimina in sinu　　　　2170
　　　　Aleremus. Arrogantia se diceret
　　　　Praecipitem ijsse? fugeret arrogantiam
　　　　Noster animus; sed ceteris periculum
　　　　Inesse vitijs crederet nullum. Bene
　　　　Itaque tacuerat singula, ut nos omnia　　　　2175
　　　　Metuere disceremus.
STEPHANUS:　　　　Hoc recte quidem.
　　　　Sed quid cavere tu potissimum jubes
　　　　Nos, Bruno?
BRUNO:　　　　Quid? Cenodoxus omnia monuit
　　　　Cavenda, dum cavere similem jusserat
　　　　Obitum. Timenda vita nobis talis est;　　　　2180
　　　　Talem necem timere serum est. Vivere

By constant fear. From eating, culture, leisure,
Discussion, reading, talking, Cenodoxus
Prevents me: sleeping, he wakes me; when awake,
He haunts me, present even in his absence.
What's left? He kills my life; makes me dread death.

STEPHEN: Bruno, the same distress afflicts my heart;
But, with my mind so torn, I do not know
What I should do.

ANDREAS: Advise us if you can.

BRUNO: I am resolved to set our hearts at rest.
Life in these perils in which others perish
Sickens and wearies.

ALL: We all feel loathing for it;
But where's a remedy?

BRUNO: Dear friends, we knew
How saintly and how virtuous a life
This man appeared to lead, whom now we've seen
Condemned to hell's extremest punishment.

ALL: He told us it himself, here as we listened.

ANDREAS: What could have been the reason for it?

BRUNO: If only
He'd told the cause more clearly! We would then
Avoid that cause, condemn that in ourselves
Which has condemned him. But by that same silence
He showed the cause more clearly; by suppressing,
More forcibly expressed it. Had he said
Hate was the cause, we would at once drive out
All hatred from our hearts, but open them
To other sins. Had he said arrogance
Had hurled him down to hell, then from our minds
We would cast arrogance, but other sins
We would consider harmless. He did well,
By specifying none, to make us learn
To fear each single one.

STEPHEN: That's true; but Bruno,
What do you bid us guard against especially?

BRUNO: What? Cenodoxus warned us against all sins
In warning us against an end like his.
A life like his is what we all should fear;
Fear of a death like his comes all too late.

Ita nolit ille, quisquis ita nolit mori.
Ah, quid putemus esse, perpeti inferas
Perenne flammas ? longa mortis taedia ?
Vermesque viperasque Conscientiae ?   2185
Et alia mille ? Malo conticescere,
Quam pauca dicere. Quicquid enim dixero,
Parum erit, nihil erit. Imo quicquid dixero,
Suave erit, amoenum erit, beatum erit; inferis
Si conferas cum supplicijs. Hoc unice   2190
Dicam; idque milliesque dicam millies,
Interrogatus de inferorum miseria;
Non creditur, non creditur, non creditur.
Testare miser; hic hic renuncia, ex tuis
Honoribus, capis levamen in tuis   2195
Cruciatibus ? Num laude capta submoves
Piceata flammarum volumina, qualibus
Nunc usque & usque & usque & usque & usque nunc
Affligeris ? Jam jam, miser, jam desinunt
Placere tibi, quae hodieque vani quaerimus   2200
Stultique mortales. Modo omnes gloriam
Sectamur; olim ut noxiam exsecrabimur.
Ah sero, sero. Nolo paenitudinem hanc
Seram opperiri: est animus antevertere,
Socij mei, jam non mei.   2205

OMNES: Sumus, erimus
   Tui.

HUGO: Itane Bruno ? tu tibi legas sidera,
   Nobis relinquas Tartara ? sequar ego, sequar.

BRUNO: Abi voluptas; hinc abite gloriae
   Cupidines; jam delicatae corporis
   Valete vestes: annuli, imo compedes,   2210
   Non annuli. Valete honores; talibus
   Remunerari si soletis praemijs
   Vestros clientes. Non meam ridebitis
   Dementiam; ridebo vestram.

HUGO: Cedite
   Opes, abite gloriae, ite litterae;   2215
   Valete saecli incommoda.

BRUNO: Imo vos mei
   Salvete, jam valete socij. Perdere
   Haec malo, quam perire.

To avoid that death, we must avoid that life.
Ah, who can contemplate the flames of hell
Eternally unceasing? Death's long agony?
The serpents and the stinging worms of Conscience?
A thousand other things?– I'd rather spare
All speech than name but few! For what I name
Will be too little! nothing! My description
Will be sweet bliss and blessed in comparison
With sufferings in hell. This I say only,
And will repeat a thousand, thousand times,
When asked about the torments of the damned:
No-one believes it, not a soul believes it.
Bear witness now, poor wretch, here, now proclaim:
Do any of your honours comfort you
In your dire torments? Can you, with your fame,
Beguile the fire, dispel the sheets of flame,
The burning pitch that ever, evermore
Are going to afflict you? Now, poor wretch,
The things we foolish, empty mortals seek
Please you no longer. All seek only glory,
And all will come to curse the harm it brings–
Too late! I want no part in such repentance,
Too late awaited. Mine is in advance,
My comrades– mine no longer.

ALL: Yours we are,
And shall be.

HUGO: Bruno, do you choose the heights
Alone, and leave us hell? I'll follow you.

BRUNO: Pleasure, farewell; farewell, all lust for glory;
Farewell, soft garments for my pampered body;
And farewell, rings– no, rather call them shackles,
Not rings. Farewell, all honours, if you pay
Your clients with such rewards and in such coin:
You are not going to have the laugh on me,
But I on you.

HUGO: Away with worldly wealth,
Farewell to pomp and fame and worldly learning,
Farewell, the age's ills.

BRUNO: Now my true friends,
I hail you, as I say farewell. All these
I'd rather lose than perish.

OMNES: Non recedimus.
STEPHANUS: Quocunque ducito, modo procul duxeris
          Cenodoxo, & hinc, ubi perijt.   2220
OMNES: Valete vos
          Inanitates.
ANDREAS: Sequor. Abite saeculi
          Retinacula.
OMNES: Sequimur, sequimur omnes.
BRUNO: Nihil
          Tenet abeuntem. Saccus istuc induet
          Inane, mortuale corpus. Cilicio
          Torquebitur; jejunio vexabitur,   2225
          Precibusque flagrisque cicurabitur meis;
          Ne forte me pessundet, ego pessundabo.
          Stat solitudinem asperam sectarier;
          Atque inde liberare animum, ubi perdidit
          Cenodoxus.   2230
OMNES: Idem est animus, est eademque mens.
BRUNO: Beate Rector Orbis, animos robora
          Caeptumque nostrum prospera. Tibi sedet
          Vitam dicare, consecrare, ducere.
OMNES: Valete; Mundi disperite gaudia.

ALL: We'll not leave you.

STEPHEN: Lead where you will, as long as it is far
   From Cenodoxus, and this place he died in.

ALL: Farewell, you vain delights.

ANDREAS: The age's trammels –
   Farewell. I follow.

ALL: As we all do.

BRUNO: Nothing
   Can hold me back. This sackcloth will enclose
   My worthless mortal frame. This shirt of hair
   Will mortify my flesh, which shall be racked
   With fasting, tamed by prayer and scourged with blows:
   I'll ruin it, lest it should ruin me.
   I am resolved to seek the harshest wilderness
   And thus set free my soul, now I have seen
   How Cenodoxus lost his.

ALL: Heart and mind,
   We are at one with you.

BRUNO: Almighty Ruler,
   Strengthen our hearts and prosper our intent.
   To you we vow and dedicate our lives.

ALL: Vanish and perish, worldly joys. Farewell.

NOTES

References, except where stated, are to line numbers.

p. 29, To the Reader. It is not clear if this preface was written by Bidermann or by the editor of the *Ludi Theatrales*.

I, i. The names of Bidermann's characters are often significant. Mariscus may be derived from 'marisca', a large inferior kind of fig, or 'mariscus', a kind of rush. Dama occurs as a slave's name in Horace, *Satires*, I, 6, 38.

25–35. This is based on a fragment quoted by Gellius and ascribed by him, with reservations, to Plautus, cf. *Noctes Atticae*, III, iii.

49. *scelus* is a term of abuse found in Plautus and Terence. Bidermann borrows many words and turns of phrase from these and other classical authors, and it hardly seems profitable to give chapter and verse for them. Tarot, op. cit., gives many references. I am also greatly indebted to Professor Dr D. Kuijper, Fzn, University of Amsterdam, for much help in tracing obscure references and explaining obscure allusions. Bidermann shows throughout a wide and detailed knowledge of classical authors. The point is that, although he draws on them at will, his language still retains a freshness and directness and is not merely a mosaic of learned allusions.

85. Bromius. A mock heroic name for a cook. It is one of the names applied to Bacchus.

108 ff. This comedy of false directions is used more than once by Bidermann (cf. *Philemon*, I, ix) to mirror the serious theme of a man who is on the wrong course.

115 ff. Bidermann follows Plautus in concocting these names (cf. *Miles Gloriosus*). Hoplitodromus, from ὁπλίτης and δρόμος means the 'heavily armed running man', cf. Pliny, 35, 71. Megaloperiphronesterus is compounded of μεγάλο and φρόνησις and means someone who is high-spirited or haughty. Pyrgopolitoxia is probably formed from πύργος, tower; πόλις, city; τόξον, bow; and means 'city towers full of bows'. It is not clear how much sense lurks behind the nonsense.

131. Cretans were in ancient times considered born liars–'lie like a trooper'.

I, ii. Hypocrisis, ὑπόκρῐσις, 'the playing a part', and hence very appropriately linked with Cenodoxus. The imagery is continued in l.210.

142. Lake Avernus was supposed to be near the entrance to the lower world, and Avernus is used to mean the infernal regions. Bidermann uses many such classical terms to indicate heaven and hell. Our translation retains some, but tends, particularly in the fifth act, to substitute Christian for classical terminology.

152. Hasta Pelias. The spear of Achilles, so-called because its shaft came from Mt Pelion, was used by Achilles to heal the wound of Telephos (Ovid, *Met.* 13, 109, *Her.*, 3, 126).

175–188, 204–205. These lines are crucial. Cenodoxus' 'virtue' is sin, and he is unaware of his hypocrisy.

I, iii. Philautia, φιλαυτια, self-love. Cenodoxus does not actually see Self-Love. The apparent dialogue is in reality a monologue. Cenodoxus here shows all the attributes of the Pharisee. The virtues he enumerates are those of the stoic. His presumption reaches its height in l.276.

I, iv. Labeo, 'one who has large lips'. Naso, 'large-nosed'. Dropax, δρῶπαξ, a pitch-plaster, depilatory. Smilax, σμῖλαξ, a yew, or convolvulus.

I, v. Cenodoxophylax. -phylax, φύλαξ, 'guardian', 'keeper'; his guardian angel.

384/385. An example of the leitmotif use of 'scire' and 'nescire'.

393. Tityos, a giant, son of Jupiter, slain by Apollo with arrows for his attempt on the chastity of Latona, and made to lie over a vast area of the infernal regions, where a vulture kept feeding on his liver, which is constantly reproduced.

403. He scatters improving texts, cf. ll. 430, 605 ff.

420/421. Panurgus underlines man's free-will.

II, i. Philaretus, φιλαρετυς, 'fond of virtue'. Bidermann's pessimism is reflected in Guarinus' criticisms of the age.

502. ad Philedemonem. I am greatly indebted to Professor Kuijper for his help in elucidating the meaning of this name. Professor Kuijper has established (Humanistica Lovaniensia XXI) that Philedemones comes from 'a man devoted to learning'. Bidermann will have found the word in Popma's 1607 edition of Cicero's *Ad Atticum*, and will not therefore have used it in the 1602 Augsburg version of *Cenodoxus*. He plays on the meaning of the name in line 506, 'si litteras amas'.

536/537. Tabulae publicae. A public register of debts exhibited in the ancient Roman treasury.

568. Pun on 'edis' and 'edes', one of several puns in the play.

578. Dama, in praising Cenodoxus for the sake of food, is resorting to the behaviour he accuses Mariscus of in I, i.

597/598. Jovem Lapidem. The statue of Jupiter at the Capitol, cf. Cic., *Fam.*, 7, 12, 2; Gell., 1, 21, 4.

605. Wisdom 5, verse 8; Old Testament (Vulgate).

606. Isaiah 37, verse 29.

608. Proverbs 16, verse 5.

637. The theme of asking too late anticipates the Navegus scenes, especially l.766 ff.

II, v. Navegus, ναυηγός, 'shipwrecked', 'stranded' (Latin 'naufragus').

653. Fames, being a feminine noun, is 'queen'.

662 ff. A good example of Bidermann's comedy, with its serious under-
tones.

676. Lustrum. A quinquennial purificatory sacrifice or expiatory offering; also used in connection with paying taxes. Perhaps the
religious, propitiatory aspect has some reference to Cenodoxus.

II, vi. Exoristus, ἐξόριστος, 'banished', 'expelled'. Ptochus, πτωχός,
'one who crouches, cringes, a beggar'. This scene, with its
echoes of Matthew, 6, 1–4, and Luke, 18, 1–14, the story of the
Pharisee and the Publican, is one of the crucial scenes of the
play. Cenodoxus shows himself as a Pharisee, and his hypocrisy
appears more conscious and calculating. His self-righteousness
appears most clearly in lines 699–708. Lines 696–699 link up
with the judgement scenes of Act v. Navegus here corresponds
to the Publican.

721. Lauduinus. It was not clear at the time Bidermann was writing
whether the name of Bruno's companion should be Landuinus,
Lauduinus, or Laudwinus. It seems clear that Bidermann
preferred the latter two versions, which are virtually identical,
and in fact almost without exception wrote Laudwinus. I am
grateful to Professor Kuijper for his scholarly help in this matter.

767. Euclio. The name of the miser in Plautus, *Aulularia*.

769. Chaldaeus. The Chaldaeans were distinguished for their knowledge of astronomy and astrology.

773 f. Cf. Virgil, *Aeneid*, 6, 417 f.

778. Megaera and 779 Tisyphone, two of the Furies.

II, viii. Dorus, the name of a character in Terence, *Eunuchus*. Dromus,
δρόμος, 'course', 'race', 'racecourse'. Cleptes, κλέπτης, 'thief'.
Aesculapius, the son of Apollo and the nymph Coronis, deified
after his death on account of his great knowledge of medicine,
father of Machaon and Podalyrius (cf. IV, i.).

800. Aesculapius is fooled by Cenodoxus, just as he is by the thief.

838. Laverna. The patron goddess of gain, and hence especially of
rogues and thieves.

862 f. This is Tarot's emendation of the text (op. cit., p. 187) and clearly
makes good sense.

II, ix. Rusticus, a man from the country, peasant. Some of the comedy
with the hard-hearing countryman is a little laboured; but the
relevance of the scene is obvious.

926 ff. nescius. Again the lack of awareness of Cenodoxus is emphasised.

960 ff. The *Everyman* motif. The guardian angel shows Cenodoxus the
book of his sins.

983. Erebus. The lower world.

1000. This line succinctly gives the reason for Cenodoxus' damnation.

1003. Tonans. God of thunder, applied to Jupiter: pagan terminology used in a Christian context. Cenodoxus is still unconscious of his guilt.

1018. Laconicum. A sweating-room, a sweating-bath, Cicero, *Att.*, 4, 10, 2, Celsus 2, 17.

1051. Proserpina. Daughter of Ceres and Jupiter, wife of Pluto, who carried her away to the infernal regions.

1052. Aeacus. Son of Jupiter by Europa, on account of his just government made judge in the lower regions, with Minos and Rhadamanthus.

1074f. St Antony of Egypt, ?251–356 and St Macarius of Egypt, c.300–c.390, both retreated to the desert. Cf. *Vita Antonii* by St Athanasius. Bruno will follow their example, not Cenodoxus.

1093f. This makes it quite clear that Self-Love is invisible to Mariscus.

1108ff. In classical myth sleep had two doors in the underworld through which dreams found their way. True dreams went through the door made of horn, false dreams through the door made of ivory. The elm harboured false dreams. Cf. Virgil, *Aeneid*, vi, 282–284, 893–896.

1119. bisextus. A leap year, so called because February 24 (*VI* Kal. Mart.) was doubled.

1169. Cf. the final scene of *Oedipus Colonneus*.

1233. prodromi. North-northeast winds that blow eight days before the rising of the dog-star, cf. Cicero, *Att.* 16, 6, 1. Could be translated as 'harbingers', but the cold winds of hell were a mediaeval concept, cf. the Anglo-Saxon poem *The Later Genesis*, l.315.

IV, i. Tarot, op. cit., 193f., has valuable notes showing how Bidermann draws on Celsus, *De medicina*, for the details of the doctors' procedure and prescriptions. The eight books on medicine form part of the 20-volume encyclopaedia written by Celsus during 14–27 A.D.

1316. inter & Saxum, & Sacrum. A classical proverb, 'to stand between the victim and the knife', 'between the devil and the deep'. The outcome depends on the choice man makes. This passage is very reminiscent of the atmosphere of the *Spiritual Exercises* (see Introduction).

1325ff. Cenodoxus is urged to bear pain like a stoic.

1372ff. The irony of these stoic sentiments is only too apparent.

1430ff. The fact that Cenodoxus does not know (again the verb 'nescire') how he has sinned is once more stressed – so subtle is the sin of pride in cloaking itself in virtue.

1444. This line is interrupted by the four lines of the chorus. The complete line therefore reads 'Sint hostibus . . . Jam machinationibus.' In the same way line 1451 is split into two by the interpolated four lines of the chorus, lines 1452/5. The first line of the first verse of the chorus, line 1445, is a direct quote from Seneca, *Apocolocyntosis*, 12, 2, 1.

1505–1514. The choice facing Cenodoxus is here most clearly put.

IV, vi. In this scene Bidermann again draws on Celsus, *De medicina* (cf. Tarot, op. cit., p. 198).

1560/1561. Irony is again apparent in this mention of a 'sanctity of a new kind'.

1569. quid moraris emori? This is a quote from Catullus, lii.

1575. Phasallioth appears here, though Bidermann does not list his name at the beginning of the scene.

1579. Cocytus. A river of the Lower World.

1716. This recalls to mind the Navegus scenes.

1723. This paradox pinpoints the sin of Cenodoxus.

1822. Christ allows Himself a play on words, 'moveri' and 'amoveri'.

1835. Cf. Marlowe, *Doctor Faustus*, scene v, 'The god thou servest is thine own appetite'.

1998ff. Bruno's words echo the sentiments of Guarinus in II, i.

2010. castra. Cf. Ignatius, *Spiritual Exercises*, Meditation on Two Standards.

2035ff. The instruments of Christ's Passion would doubtless be shown on the stage, e.g. nails, hammer, spear, sponge.

2056. Cf. St Luke 23, 30.

2072f. To suit the needs of scansion the lines should be written:
> Mortalium. JUSTO DEI JUDICIO
> DAMNATUS SUM. Perennes eheu jam rogos

2090ff. These lines emphasise the fact that Bruno and his companions have no idea why Cenodoxus is damned. Cf. 2166ff.

2106f. Meichel, in his 1635 German translation, says in the introduction to this scene that the drink consists of sulphur and pitch. The Munich (1609) and Ingolstadt (1607) Programmes of the *Cenodoxus* productions also give these details.

2122. Phlegethon was a river in the Lower World which ran with fire instead of water.

2127. salarium. Cf. *Romans*, 6, 23, 'the wages of sin'.

2208ff. Note the triumphant scorn with which Bruno rejects the world. His is no weak escapism.

2214. dementia, 'insanity', 'madness'. This picks up the insanity motif of the Mariscus scenes, giving a serious twist to the comic theme.

2216. saecli incommoda. cf. Catullus, 14, 23.

BIBLIOGRAPHY

Jakob Bidermann, *Ludi Theatrales*, 1666, ed. Rolf Tarot, 2 vol. Tübingen 1967.

Jakob Bidermann, *Cenodoxus*, ed. Rolf Tarot, Tübingen 1963.

D. G. Dyer, *Jacob Bidermann. A Seventeenth-Century German Jesuit Dramatist*, Diss., Cambridge 1950.

Rolf Tarot, *Jakob Bidermanns 'Cenodoxus'*, Diss., Cologne 1960.

Julius Rütsch, 'Die Bedeutung Jacob Bidermanns', in *Trivium*, Vol. 5, 1960.

Max Wehrli, 'Bidermanns *Cenodoxus*' in *Das deutsche Drama*, ed. Benno von Wiese, Vol. 1, Düsseldorf 1958.

Hans Pörnbacher, 'Jacob Bidermann (1578–1639)', in *Lebensbilder aus dem Bayerischen Schwaben*, 1973.

Backer-Sommervogel, *Bibliothèque de la Compagnie de Jésus*, 9 vols., Paris 1890–1900.

Heinz Kindermann, *Theatergeschichte Europas*, vols. 2 & 3, Salzburg 1959.

Ignatius Loyola, *The Spiritual Exercises*, trans. Thomas Corbishley S.J., 1963.

Johannes Müller, *Das Jesuitendrama in den Ländern deutscher Zunge*, 2 vols., Augsburg 1930.

New Catholic Encyclopedia, 15 vols., New York 1967.